Sonderband
Special Issue

Voluntaris – Zeitschrift für Freiwilligendienste und
zivilgesellschaftliches Engagement /
Voluntaris – Journal of Volunteer Services and Civic Engagement

Editorial Committee:

Editorial Office:

Voluntaris, c/o Professur für Sozialpolitik, Benjamin Haas, Universität zu Köln,
Albertus-Magnus-Platz, D-50923 Köln, redaktion@voluntaris.de

Rebecca Tiessen | Benjamin J. Lough | Tiffany Laursen
Khursheed Sadat (Eds.)

Innovations in Gender Equality and Women's Empowerment

Understanding the Role of International Development Volunteers as Transnational Actors

The Deutsche Nationalbibliothek lists this publication in the Deutsche Nationalbibliografie; detailed bibliographic data are available on the Internet at http://dnb.d-nb.de

ISBN   978-3-8487-7105-9 (Print)
            978-3-7489-2495-1 (ePDF)

British Library Cataloguing-in-Publication Data
A catalogue record for this book is available from the British Library.

ISBN   978-3-8487-7105-9 (Print)
            978-3-7489-2495-1 (ePDF)

Library of Congress Cataloging-in-Publication Data
Tiessen, Rebecca / Lough, Benjamin J. / Laursen, Tiffany / Sadat, Khursheed
Innovations in Gender Equality and Women's Empowerment
Understanding the Role of International Development Volunteers
as Transnational Actors
Rebecca Tiessen / Benjamin J. Lough / Tiffany Laursen / Khursheed Sadat (Eds.)
164 pp.
Includes bibliographic references.

ISBN   978-3-8487-7105-9 (Print)
            978-3-7489-2495-1 (ePDF)

1st Edition 2021
© The Authors

Published by
Nomos Verlagsgesellschaft mbH & Co. KG
Waldseestraße 3–5 | 76530 Baden-Baden
www.nomos.de

Production of the printed version:
Nomos Verlagsgesellschaft mbH & Co. KG
Waldseestraße 3–5 | 76530 Baden-Baden

ISBN   978-3-8487-7105-9 (Print)
ISBN   978-3-7489-2495-1 (ePDF)
DOI   https://doi.org/10.5771/9783748924951

Onlineversion
Nomos eLibrary

TABLE OF CONTENTS

CONCLUSION

INTRODUCTION

Innovations in Gender Equality and Women's Empowerment: Understanding the Role of International Development Volunteers as Transnational Actors

Rebecca Tiessen and Benjamin J. Lough

This special issue of *Voluntaris* helps us understand the distinctive contributions of international development volunteers (IDVs) to gender equality and women's empowerment (GEWE) programming in the Global South. Building on critical development theory, feminist theory, subaltern studies and human capabilities literature, this collection assesses the complex roles and impacts of IDVs as transnational actors on partner organization programming and the promotion of gender equality outcomes.

Global disparities and limited opportunities for women continue to catch them in traps of inequality. As articulated in Sustainable Development Goal (SDG) #5, achieving gender equality and empowering all women and girls is essential to accelerating and achieving sustainable development. Gender equality is more than a basic human right, it also creates a multiplier effect with the capacity to magnify all other development outcomes. Indeed, the thematic priority of gender equality chosen for this special issue emerged from previous research as a development outcome that results in heightened capacity development in international volunteering programs needed to achieve other SDGs.

Previous research conducted by the special issue editor(s) resulted in an improved understanding about how diverse forms of international volunteering are associated with capacity building and development outcomes from the perspective of partner organizations (see Lough/Tiessen 2018; Lough/Tiessen/Lasker 2018; Tiessen/Grantham/Lough 2018; Tiessen/Lough 2018). However, the exploratory research included in these earlier publications also uncovered additional gaps of express interest to volunteer-involving organizations. Among these diverse organizations, Volunteer Cooperation Agencies (VCAs) were specifically interested in understanding how the distinctive characteristics of volunteering can enhance or inhibit local capacities in pursuit of SDG targets – particularly in areas such as gender equality. Furthermore, this previous research provided a high degree of quantitative findings that highlighted overarching trends and experiences but lacked sufficient qualitative information about the nature of the partnerships and collaborations in support of specific programming strategies and outcomes, especially in the area of gender equality programming.

While gross inequalities still exist in access to paid employment, equal opportunities in the labour market, equal rights to land and property ownership, and equal gender division in relation to unpaid care and domestic work, this research shines a light on how IDVs address these challenges as they expose and advocate for equality in their direct engagements with host communities, as well as their advocacy efforts abroad.

The data collected for this special issue underscore several core ways that IDVs contribute to GEWE in areas such as: capacity building, intercultural relations, women-focused versus gender-focussed programming, perceptions of feminism, social innovation and women's economic empowerment, addressing masculinities and the inclusion of men and boys, women's political and economic participation, and grass roots impacts.

Employing ten country case studies (Ghana, Kenya, Malawi, Tanzania, Senegal, Ghana, Nepal, Vietnam, Guatemala and Peru), the individual papers included in this special issue summarize data collected between 2018-2019 and analysed between 2019-2020. The data were collected and analysed by emerging Northern and Southern scholars that include locally based researchers in the Global South, international students, and Canadian researchers. These teams of transnational researchers coded and analyzed a full set of interview transcripts and coded the material to identify common themes through content analysis. Several of these researchers then summarized their analyses into the chapters that became the body of this special collection. The research process encompassed a collaborative research design, shared data analysis and the co-creation of knowledge with practitioner organizations including Volunteer Cooperation Agencies (VCAs) that are part of Canada's Volunteer Cooperation Program (VCP) as well as partner organizations that receive volunteers in the Global South. This collaborative research design and writing process underscore the dynamic and reciprocal ways that knowledge about – and commitments to – gender equality are shared through transnational activities and development programming involving IDVs.

1. Introduction

Addressing gender inequality in international development requires broad ranging commitments from diverse organizations and individuals. In this collection, we examine the experiences of partner organizations and communities in the Global South who have worked with IDVs and their reflections on IDV support to GEWE. International development volunteers are distinguished from alternative forms of international volunteering for "international understanding" with a focus on the hosting community or organization as the prime beneficiary, with key aims of empowerment and capacity building (Lough/Tiessen 2018). Throughout the papers in this collection, the role and impact of IDVs are viewed through a transnational actor lens, emphasizing the relationships that emerge through the interactions between IDVs and partner organization staff.

This introductory paper provides an overview of IDVs as development actors: their roles, functions and affiliations. We were particularly interested in learning about Canadian IDVs who are taking part in Canada's Volunteer Cooperation Program (VCP) and the role of the VCP in facilitating IDV connections with partner organizations as part of their broader programmatic objectives. However, partner organizations provided a number of examples of IDVs from a large range of countries and therefore the data are not reflective solely of Canadian transnational actors specifically. The interviews also focused on priorities guiding the VCP and other foreign aid funding as outlined by Global Affairs Canada (GAC) through its 2017 foreign aid policy titled *Canada's Feminist International Assistance Policy* (FIAP). Data collected during interviews provided insights specific to knowledge about Canada's FIAP.

The thematic focus on women and girls is a core priority of GAC. Canada's FIAP (GAC 2017) is committed to ensuring no less than 95 percent of Canadian bilateral aid advances gender equality and promotes the empowerment of women and girls by 2021-2022 (GAC 2017). The Government of Canada recognizes that the lack of women's economic opportunities comes at great cost to economic prosperity and growth (GAC 2017). Thus, concerns for gender equality have been longstanding issues for critical discourse (e.g. postcolonial feminism) and have remained an ongoing commitment at every major global summit in the past three years. To better inform these outcomes, the research contained in this collection asked communities to specifically reflect on how the priorities of FIAP influence their lives.

This paper then turns to an overview of the methodology employed in designing and carrying out the empirical research, including the specific methods of data collection and analysis used to understand the themes and conclusions that emerged in the separate papers included in this collection. We end this paper with a brief overview of individual papers included in the special collection. This roadmap to the issue reviews the key arguments and messages of each of the papers and summarizes how these papers advance our knowledge in line with specific thematic areas of focus in relation to the role and impact of IDVs as transnational actors promoting GEWE in collaboration with partner organizations in the Global South. Taken together these papers illustrate the distinctive contributions of IDVs and the significance of transnational interactions for partner organizations working together to promote GEWE.

1.1 The Role of IDVs as Actors in Transnational Relations

IDVs involved in transnational relations engage in international relations as non-state actors in important ways (Hagel 2011; Clarke 2005). Although diverse types of international volunteers may engage with transnational relations with a focus on "international understanding" (see Lough/Tiessen 2018), we are interested in better understanding the role of IDVs, who prioritize the needs and capacities of hosting communities and organizations as their primary target.

The concept of transnational relations is an encompassing term that covers a range of interactions but with a specific emphasis on human agency (Risse 2013). Nye and Keohane (1971: 332) defined transnational relations as: "Regular interactions across national boundaries when at least one actor is a non-state agent". The processes and forces of globalization have facilitated growing transnational linkages across diverse agents including civil society actors, "encouraging greater civil society engagement in some areas of Canadian foreign policy decision-making after 1968" (Macdonald 2018: 359). One of the distinctive features of transnational relations, however, is the way that globalization is viewed from – and enacted as – "globalization from below" (Della Porta/Massimiliano/Mosca/Reiter 2006), or an 'actor-centred' approach (Risse 2013) and focuses attention on the role of transnational actors "in social policymaking, encouraging critical engagement and examination of their behavior and activities" (Shriwise 2020: 34).

Transnational relations are also characterized by largely informal ties as well as the "diffusion of ideas and information, with little formal organizational substance" (Macdonald 2018). These relations, however, are linked to the expansion of global civil society which is deemed "a crucial component for championing positive transformative change, including gender equality, inclusion, respect for diversity and human rights, peace and security, and development" (GAC 2017: no page number).

Scholarship on transnational relations has also highlighted the role of transnational actors in norm diffusion (Landolt 2004) and knowledge production (Haas/Repenning, 2018). Asking the question: "How do norms travel?", Zwingle (2012: 115) calls for more sophisticated analyses of the roles and impacts of transnational actors, pointing out that "global to local flows of norms inherent in most of the global norm diffusion literature is simplistic". When it comes to the transnational diffusion of knowledge and norms in comparison with intra-national relations, unequal power relations between stakeholders in the Global North and Global South require a more critical reflection on the nature and impact of postcolonial power structures.

While transnational actors, and IDVs in particular, can participate in diverse forms of norm diffusion from human rights to democratic governance, the focus in this collection is on norm and knowledge diffusion through transnational relationships, with a focus on feminist principles and the values of gender equality. Transnational interactions between IDVs and partner organization staff in the Global South highlight how understandings of GEWE are shaped over time. IDVs are linked to enhanced confidence for GEWE programming and are known to offer alternative strategies, model different gender practices, and shape attitudes and behaviours related to gender equality (Tiessen/Rao/Lough 2021). Given concerns about cultural imperialism, norm diffusion around gender equality and feminist values is often met with resistance and reinterpretation in foreign communities. In other contexts, however, the diffusion of gender equality as a fundamental human right is widely embraced and accepted as an effective method for allyship and in the promotion of changes to discriminatory norms in pursuit of equal opportunities for women and girls.

1.2 Defining IDVs

Devereux (2008: 359 – 360) describes the distinctive characteristics of IDVs as volunteers with humanitarian motivations; a commitment to reciprocal benefit; willingness to live work under local conditions and with a long-term commitment; local accountability and North-South partnership; and emphasis on tackling causes rather than symptoms of poverty in their work. Supervision of the day-to-day work of IDVs is performed by the local organization and IDVs are primarily accountable to this local organization.

With this baseline definition in mind, a simple definition of international development volunteering is complicated by the diverse program modalities that exist. It is important to distinguish between the different forms of transnational relations that are often characterized in terms of directional flows such as South-South or North-South or South-North volunteering. Other important differences include the length of the volunteer placement. While many IDVs live abroad for one year or longer, short term but skilled volunteers of six months or less can also contribute substantially to development (see Lough/Tiessen 2018).

One important distinction that separates the forms of international volunteering, however, is the differences between learner-centred or development-centred placements. Some of the IDVs discussed during interviews would fall under the category of learning-focused because they were students or recent graduates with limited professional skills to share at the time of their IDV placement. For the sample studied in this special issue we consider IDVs who fit the category of North-South volunteers who generally have professional skills to share, and, for the most part, are Canadian citizens travelling abroad. Partner organization staff were asked to share their experiences of working with IDVs. Distinguishing between the nationalities of IDVs can be challenging for some organizations since they may host volunteers from multiple countries. During interviews, partner organization staff were asked to try to think of their particular experiences working with Canadian IDVs and to consider the role and impact of IDVs who were placed through Canada's Volunteer Cooperation Program (VCP).

Given the importance of the VCP program to the majority of the volunteer placements, we provide a short summary of it here. Since the 1960s, the Government of Canada has sent tens of thousands of international volunteers to work in development projects around the world through Canada's VCP. Between 2015 and 2020, The Volunteer Cooperation Program (VCP), supported by the Government of Canada, funded twelve IDV projects managed by 15 Volunteer Cooperation Agencies (VCAs) to facilitate volunteer placements for 10,000 IDVs to more than 50 countries (Government of Canada 2020). The objectives of Canada's VCP align with the definition and distinctive characteristics of IDVs noted above including: increasing the capacity of developing-country partners to deliver sustainable development results in response to local needs; and enhancing Canadians' participation in Canada's development efforts to promote a better understanding of development challenges (Government of Canada 2018). While the Volunteer Receiving Organizations that host these volunteers complete mid- and end-term reports and evaluations of these IDV programs, these evaluations are not in the public domain. Therefore, little is known about the roles of IDVs, their positive or negative impacts, and their distinctive contributions to the delivery of programs of explicit interest to the Government of Canada, including programs with clearly-defined priorities for the promotion of gender equality.

2. Filling Gaps in Scholarship on International Development Volunteering

Research and scholarship on international development volunteering have addressed several themes worth highlighting in this collection including the pros and cons of international engagement – particularly in the case of North-South volunteering. International volunteerism can "facilitate social integration and social inclusion", encourage "cross-cultural exchange and knowledge-sharing" as well as advance the United Nations Sustainable Development Goals (SDGs) (Lough 2015: 3; Tiessen 2018: 1). Volunteers and the VCAs that facilitate their placements "develop partnerships and are able to contribute to development assistance" (Tiessen 2018: 1).

Much of the literature to date has focussed on motivations and experiences of international volunteers (Helms/McKenzie 2014; Lee/Won 2018; Lough/Xiang 2016; Johnson 2015; L. Chen/J. Chen 2011). Recently, scholarship has also highlighted the impact of IDVs, focussing on effectiveness and impact of international volunteering (Palacios 2010; Smith 2014; Trau 2015; Louiseau et al. 2016; Campbell Lehn 2015; Lough/Tiessen 2017; Lough/Tiessen/Lasker 2018). Thanks to this research, we now know much more about how diverse forms of international volunteering are associated with development outcomes (Lough/ Tiessen 2017; Lough/Tiessen/Lasker 2018; Tiessen/Grantham/Lough 2018; Tiessen/Lough 2018). On the other hand, only some of this research has incorporated the voice of community members and organizations that interact with volunteers. Previous research conducted by the special issue editors which was published in *Voluntaris* in 2018 resulted in improved understanding about how diverse forms of international volunteering are associated with capacity building and development outcomes from the perspective of partner organizations in the Global South (Lough/ Tiessen 2017; Lough et al. 2018; Tiessen/Grantham/Lough 2018; Tiessen/Lough 2018). However, the exploratory research also uncovered many additional gaps of express interest to volunteer-involving organizations. In particular, research from the perspective of partner organization staff about their experiences working with IDVs, including the relationship-building aspects of transnational interactions, as well as specific programmatic work carried out in collaboration between IDVs and partner organizations in support of GEWE remains a gap in scholarship.

2.1 Incorporating Southern Voices in IDV Scholarship

Building upon the success of the previous *Voluntaris* special issue, the goal of this collection is to further leverage the voices and the stories of Southern hosts to broaden this knowledge base. The research for this collection therefore adds to scholarship on IDVs, transnational actors, and international development; particularly the emphasis on agency of Southern partners and communities in development processes that affect their lives. Much of the theorizing on international volunteering has followed a critical theory approach (i.e., postcolonial and neoliberal critiques) that has originated from scholarship rooted in the Global North (Baillie Smith/ Laurie 2011; see Heron 2007; Georgeou/Engel 2011; Noxolo 2011; Perold et al. 2013; Tiessen/Kumar 2013). Building on existing scholarship on the human capabilities framework, our approach "underscores the potential for improved quality of life across the globe and allows for the consideration of other human capabilities and improvements stemming from good health or meaningful or loving relationships that have been linked to international volunteering" (Tiessen/ Lough/Cheung 2018:12).

Moving beyond the Northern-centric theoretical analysis of critical postcolonialism, this collection employs discursive normative theory (Nussbaum 2003; Kanbur/Shaffer 2007) and identity-based theories that highlight the importance of capacities and agency of traditionally conceived "recipients" of aid (see, in this collection, Shahadu Bitimsamli who considers masculinities; and Mpogazi and Saint-Denis who draw on empowerment scholarship). These theoretical approaches are highly relevant to practice partners in the Global South that are firmly rooted in practice realities. However, they have received very little scholarly attention in studies of international volunteering (Tiessen/Lough/Cheung 2018). Greater attention to the agency, voice and social capital of those positioned in the Global South (see Loiseau et al. 2016; Perold et al. 2013; Tiessen 2018) informs both theoretical analysis and research methodologies that consider subaltern voices (Saffari 2016; Tiessen/Grantham/Lough 2018). In employing the theoretical and methodological lens of agency and human capability, we aim for a richer analysis of the perspectives and experiences of the Global South partners who work alongside IDVs on international development programming aiming to promote gender equality.

2.2 International Volunteering as a Complementary Feminist Approach to Development Practice

Compared to other aid approaches, some scholars have described volunteering as a particularly "feminist" approach that prioritizes human and relational strategies over heavy-handed technocratic development approaches (Devereux 2010; Tiessen/Grantham/Lough 2018). Operating within a relational approach to development, IDVs complement dominant technical and market-based approaches to international development, turning away from the strict association between development and economic growth to value the enhancement of human abilities and solutions (Devereux 2008; Lewis 2006). Consistent with this approach, we aim to investigate the degree to which international development volunteering programs operate within this feminist perspective, and how international development volunteering's relational approach may help to address SDG 5 targets focused on promoting gender equality and the empowerment of women and girls. As such, the focus on gender equality and women's empowerment (GEWE) is a central area of analysis across all papers. The papers in this collection focus on a range of themes specific to GEWE including equal rights, legal protections, political participation, economic empowerment, and gender relations.

The international voluntary sector, along with the volunteers that populate this sector, are important contributors to collaborative practice through knowledge sharing and the implementation of the SDGs. Unfortunately, lack of investment into research on volunteering in development has kept the contributions of this sector hidden, understudied and undervalued (Devereux/Guse 2012; Seelig/Lough 2015). To date, only a handful of qualitative studies have investigated the complementary contributions of international volunteering—pointing to qualities such as social capital, innovation, flexibility, challenging gender norms, improving human rights awareness, and building vertical "bridges" or relational networks with higher-level actors (Devereux 2010; Lough 2014; Burns et al. 2015; Lough 2015).

This collection helps to fill these gaps. As the papers in the issue illustrate, turning international targets and commitments to gender equality into practical action requires partnerships from diverse actors working across the local-international divide. Equipped with distinctive relational motivations and attributes, international volunteering is purportedly "well-placed to create pathways to economic empowerment of women and youth" (UNV 2017: 1). Despite the contributions referenced in global practice and policy documents, the evidence base to support claims of relational complementarity from international volunteering is still weak – especially in this field. To adequately capture the relational complementary contributions of VCP to gender equality, this collection illustrates diverse ways that volunteers engage in the processes and systems directed toward local change efforts.

Theoretically, relational outcomes such as inspiration, trust, networks, cross-cultural understanding, and interpersonal skills transfers are critical complements to technical development processes (Fukuda-Parr/Lopes/Malik 2002; Lough 2015). Pathways from international volunteer engagement to end-goals such as gender equality and other SDGs depend on achieving intermediary relational outcomes such as building mediating networks, altering gender norms through interpersonal engagement in open systems, and sharing skills through capacity-building strategies. Theories that measure relationship-based processes can capture this narrative by "linking the chain of causality within each step" from intermediary outcomes to distinctive contributions (Mattero/Campbell-Patton 2008: 43). By making these causal linkages, findings within these papers document how IDVs are instrumental to GEWE and related SDG outcomes.

Throughout this collection, the impact of IDVs in support of GEWE programming considers different approaches from Women in Development (WID) to Gender and Development (GAD). In brief, WID aims to increase women's access to resources and economic development, emphasizing inclusion, participation and the fulfillment of practical needs. GAD moves beyond the mere inclusion of women to consider the systemic reasons for exclusion and marginalization; the significance of addressing strategic gender interests; to show how gender relations are influenced by the gendered division of labour (Moser 1993); and to transform the structures of power to facilitate new opportunities for participation and empowerment (Parpart 2014). As a shorthand, WID and GAD enable theoretical analyses drawing on feminist scholarship to underscore the tensions and explanatory power of critical and postcolonial feminist theory and the contributions of feminist subaltern insights in relation to "othering" (Spivak 1999; Tiessen/Baranyi 2017), as universal aspects of women's experiences, instrumentalization of women for development outcomes (Tiessen 2015), and the prospects for feminist international relations (Tiessen/Swan 2018).

These frameworks of analysis are important for making sense of the diverse approaches to GEWE programming and can be used to make sense of distinctive contributions of IDVs (skills and capacity building, relationship formation, etc.)

and results (the changes that take place in gender equality measures through the synergies created through partner organization/IDV interactions). Taken together, these theoretical approaches provide new lenses to investigate and document whether the complementary contributions of international volunteerism truly support global partnership arrangements that can achieve end-goals of GEWE and related SDG outcomes (Schech et al. 2015). The eight thematic papers in this collection offer important insights into the processes and outcomes of interactions in transnational spaces focusing on themes of diverse experiences of empowerment; locally based interpretations and cultural adaptations of feminist principles and GEWE goals and priorities; and gender relations within partner organizations and between partner organizations, IDVs and community members.

3. Methodology

The methodology employed across all the papers in this collection reinforces the goals and objectives of this project by enhancing knowledge of collaborative, reciprocal, and solidarity-oriented practice through the inclusion of Global South perspectives in the design and implementation of research. The research methodology began by enhancing the capacity of emerging scholars (senior undergraduate and graduate students from Canada and graduate students or recent graduates from countries in the Global South) to design and carry out data collection, to transcribe, analyze and organize findings, and to write up thematic papers drawing on data across all country case studies. Where possible, locally-based researchers were hired to conduct the research. Three of the researchers engaged in data-collection in partner countries are locally based researchers (graduate students or recent graduates) and a fourth researcher is an international student studying in Canada who returned to his home country for data collection. The remaining five researchers were emerging scholars (senior undergraduate or graduate students) studying in Canada.

The research team worked closely with partner organization staff in ten countries in the research plan, helping with identification of interview participants, identifying communities to visit to learn about outcomes of development programming.

The research team took a "portfolio approach" to the study of international development volunteering. Consistent with the three sets of theoretical approaches underpinning this research project: (1) the normative co-generation of knowledge through shared responsibility between international researchers and local citizens in the Global South, (2) the relational complementarity of IDVs, and (3) the gendered analysis of outcomes advanced by IDVs. Working together, the research team developed research tools, contributed to the ethics application and were listed on the research project for the purpose of ethics clearance, and analyzed new and existing data through a gender lens. Partner organizations included in the study provided feedback on the research design and interview questions to ensure the cultural appropriateness of the study design and instruments used in this study.

Qualitative interviews and focus groups were carried out in a representative sample of ten countries in Africa, Asia and Latin America where Canada's VCP is actively engaged.[1] The ten countries were selected as locations where VCAs have had long-standing commitments to sending IDVs.

Interviews were carried out with an average of two staff members per organiza-tion. One of the staff members held a senior position within the organization and the other interviewee was selected based on their experience working closely with IDVs. The interview participants included both men and women staff members. On average, 15 interviews were conducted in each of the ten countries with an equi-table representation of men and women interviewees.

The interviews were open-ended and semi-structured with a common set of guid-ing questions used across all ten countries to ensure a level of consistency between interviews but also flexibility in responding, returning to questions, elaboration, story-telling, etc. With consent from the interviewees, the interviews were audio recorded. The majority of interviews were conducted in English but in some cases, interviews were conducted in French (in Senegal) and in Spanish (in Peru and Guatemala) or in Vietnamese (in Vietnam) and translated to English during the transcription stage.

Once all interviews were transcribed, the material was coded and analyzed, each researcher reviewed the full set of transcripts and coded the material to identify common themes throughout. Additional research assistants joined some of the original research team in the reviewing and coding of data, and these roles trans-formed into authorship of papers in this collection. Several themes emerged through the process of content analysis and those themes became the focus of this collection.

Document review of VCA reports and Government of Canada mid-term and end-of-cycle reports (obtained through research placements in-country) was also con-ducted to provide additional context and insight. To conduct the document review, all authors were provided the country summary reports. Each author reviewed the summary reports in line with the themes specific to their papers to find key words, ideas, and themes that fit the general theme of their respective papers. Information was compiled into thematic-specific notes and trends were examined across sub-themes. The authors then used specific quotes from those findings to provide rich examples and nuance to their papers.

---

1   Two in West Africa (Ghana and Senegal), four in East and South-East Africa (Uganda, Kenya, Tanzania and Malawi); two in Asia (Nepal and Vietnam) and two in Latin America (Peru and Guatemala).

As this collection will illustrate, the data collected across the ten countries found that overall IDVs are important transnational actors working in partnership with Global South hosts to achieve common goals and priorities for gender equality and women's empowerment. The papers in this collection also provide important insights into common and shared goals of GEWE and some of the strategies and priorities needed to support improved GEWE programming in collaboration with partner organizations and local communities in partner organizations.

The findings from across the ten case studies provides valuable aggregate information to inform a deeper analysis of trends and impacts of gender equality programming outcomes resulting from interactions between IDVs and partner organization staff. Documentation of the role and impact of IDVs in the promotion of GEWE were catalogued in relation to the frames and approaches noted above and the tools to analyse the research findings were co-designed by the lead research team as well as and emerging scholars from Canada, the USA, and the Global South during the data analysis phase.

4. Overview of Papers in the Collection[2]

In the paper titled *'Capacity Building and Capability Development: Understanding the Relations of Power and Exchange Between International Development Volunteers and Partner Organizations and Communities'*, Sadat explores the collaborative process of capacity building and capabilities development among IDVs, partner organizations, and host communities in the Global South. Unique to her work is the focus on the power dynamics that characterize this transnational interaction between IDVs and partner organizations, and its influence on the quality of capacity building and capabilities development that takes place. Using the capabilities approach (Sen 1999; Nussbaum 2011) as a frame and drawing on data across all ten countries, she underscores the reciprocal and mutually beneficial nature of capacity building and capabilities development. The author shows that through their sustained interactions, IDVs built partner organizations' capacity through several measures like skills transfer, and technical and intercultural knowledge sharing while simultaneously gaining practical context-relevant knowledge and skills on GEWE from partner organizations.

Rouhani's paper, *'Creating cosmopolitan identities in transnational spaces to advance gender equality'*, highlights how IDVs' transnational relations with partner organizations in transnational spaces effects a shift in the latter's cosmopolitan and global citizenship perspectives as it relates to gender equality and empowerment. Evidence from the ten country case studies suggests that this cross-cultural

---

2   See information about the authors at the end of the special issue.

interaction between IDVs and partner organizations (one based on reciprocity and mutual learning) was instrumental in introducing novel ideas that positively reshaped both parties' feminist values and perspectives, and consequently their cosmopolitan identities and global citizenship. Not only were partner organizations' capacities built through this interaction, but the process was also perceived to be an equal cosmopolitan exchange of values, norms, ideas and knowledge on gender equality and empowerment.

The third paper in this collection, *'Organizational Commitments to Gender Equality Programming: Resistance, Externalizing and Opportunities for Gender Mainstreaming'*, examines GEWE programming and IDV support for gender mainstreaming in development organizations. Lan Nguyen examines gender dynamics within development organizations as a factor for considering GEWE outcomes in beneficiary communities. The paper highlights the subordinate position of gender mainstreaming on partner organizations' agendas and their neglect of the intersectional and structural dimension of gender inequality. Nguyen's paper examines IDVs' contributions to – and the persistent challenges to – organizational change and gender mainstreaming faced by partner organizations.

In *'Strings Attached? How Global South partner organizations' perceptions of feminism shape their relationships with Feminist Foreign Policy Donors from the Global North'*, Laursen probes into partner organizations' perceptions of donor priorities and mandates, particularly Canada's Feminist International Assistance Policy. Using Coston's (1998) analytical framework, Laursen shows that partner organizations had varied levels of knowledge about the policies and varied capacities to benefit from the resources available through the policies. Her study also highlights that donor feminist priorities have also helped to amplify GEWE on the ground, but partner organizations have to negotiate the power differentials that characterize their relationship with donors. Specifically, she shows how partner organizations strategically exert their agency and autonomy when their feminist values were at odds with those espoused by Northern donors due to the latter's contextual disconnect.

'Social Innovation and Economic Empowerment as Opportunities for Gender Equality and Women's Empowerment in International Development Volunteering' by Tiessen, Laursen and Lough focuses on the contribution of IDVs to GEWE and social innovation programming in partner organizations and their host communities. The authors show that across the ten country case studies, IDVs initiated several innovative measures in the operations of partner organizations that positively impacted women's inclusion and participation in empowerment programs and the wider labour market. Such innovations, for example, targeted and alleviated structural barriers to women's participation such as their care work burden. In addition, partner organizations benefitted from IDVs' broad range of knowledge and skills

to enhance the design and implementation of their GEWE policies and programs. The authors emphasize the need for local sensitivities and knowledge of cultures and communities to be effective, strategic, and impactful.

Using a transnational feminist lens, Shahadu Bitamsimli examines the experiences of partner organizations as they work with IDVs to deliver GEWE programs in the Global South. In *Transnational Feminism as a Lens for Exploring Resistance, Cooperation and Collaboration with International Development Volunteers in Gender Equality and Women's Empowerment Programs,* the author uncovers the harmonies and tensions inherent in partner organizations' relations with IDVs, and the range of strategies employed by partner organizations to navigate them. The exercise of agency echoes across Shadadu's account of partner organizations' strategies of resistance, cooperation, and collaboration across the country case studies. His paper centers on the important role that partner organizations and IDVs transnational engagement can play in tackling hostilities and resistance to the transformation of oppressive gender attitudes and institutions. It also notes that the realization of feminist goals is significantly tied to the recruitment of male allies to push the GEWE agenda. On this latter point, Shahadu Bitamsimli argues that male IDVs can exhibit alternative masculinities that transcend traditional gender roles which can then alter the patriarchal perspectives and attitudes of local communities in favour of GEWE.

In *Women's Political Participation, Activism and Advocacy to Promote Gender Equality Facilitated by IDVs,* Mpogazi is concerned with highlighting how IDVs support women's political participation as they mobilize in the grassroots to engage with both state and non-state political structures and networks. The author draws on data from across the country case studies to show how IDVs promoted women's political empowerment and leadership by providing mentorship and social support to women; providing technical assistance for gender advocacy; and equipping partner organizations with empirical evidence and skills to support their activism and advocacy on women's issues. The analysis also emphasizes the importance of informal grassroots organizing which is outside the formal political domain but equally necessary for realizing gender equality and empowerment. As well, the author calls for critical reflexivity on the part of IDVs for more effective and contextually relevant support to women's political participation and empowerment.

In *International Volunteers as Empowerment Agents: Challenges and Opportunities of IDV Contributions to Women's Empowerment Programs in Partner Communities,* Saint-Denis contends that the conceptualization of "empowerment" that IDVs promote in the Global South is limited and depoliticized by its neoliberal framing. She argues that empowerment has been reduced from a political concept to a buzzword concerned with economic liberalization of women through the transfer of skills and resources. Nonetheless, the author opines that IDVs can still contribute positively to empowerment by prompting transformation in local attitudes and perspectives on gender equality through the exchange of knowledge in formal and informal spaces. The author also acknowledges that IDVs helped to foster women's economic empowerment by combining strategies to promote critical analyses of structures of inequality that lead to economic inequality with relevant training and workshops to build their professional and entrepreneurial capacities. As challenges to IDVs' contribution to women's empowerment, Saint-Denis identifies cultural tensions which manifest when IDVs attempt to impose Western feminist ideals in the local context and when they dismiss local gender norms.

5. Conclusion

The collection concludes with a summary of the papers in the collection, recapping and synthesizing the key arguments presented by the authors in this special issue. Okoli situates the findings in the broader literature by discussing their implications for international development volunteering and GEWE programming. The author also recommends the prioritization of cultural orientation for IDVs before and during their placement; critical reflexivity in IDVs' interactions with locals; and IDVs increased engagement with local feminist scholarship and organizations in their attempts to promote GEWE programming. Okoli suggests that along with partner organizations' deliberate cultural orientation efforts, improved IDV preparation can facilitate cultural sensitivity and learning among IDVs and enhanced programmatic outcomes for partner organizations. This cultural learning can build on the mutual exchange of information and the generative nature of learning that transpires during collaborative and transnational work on GEWE, which can lead to the production and sharing of "transnational" knowledge.

Together, the papers in this collection provide an overview of the unique interactions and synergies created through the transnational relationships forged while IDVs collaborate with partner organizations in gender equality and women's empowerment programming. Across the ten countries in this study, important insights are gained about the nature of the distinctive contributions made by IDVs. Examples provided in the eight papers in this collection demonstrate the significance of the cultural contexts in which transnational actors operate and the specific strategies employed by partner organizations as they negotiate change in their collaborations with IDVs. The findings highlight valuable information about diverse contributions to empowerment (political, social, and economic) and deepen our understanding of gender relations to consider gender equality and empowerment in relation to structural realities and root causes of gender inequality.

The research also considers the value and impact of gender-focused social innovations, and the potential for transnational relations to enhance capacity building and global civic engagement specific to gender equality.

Acknowledgements

Drs Tiessen and Lough wish to thank the Social Sciences and Humanities Research Council of Canada (SSHRC) for their generous support in funding that facilitated data collection in ten countries between 2018-2019, and for resources to support the open access of this publication. We also wish to thank the external reviewers for their helpful feedback on earlier drafts.

To conduct this research and to prepare these papers, we worked with a team of dedicated researchers from several countries. We are grateful to all members of the team who played important roles throughout the data collection, analysis and writing stages. In addition to the chapter authors, we also wish to thank the larger team who helped with the data collection and analysis for this collection. Many thanks to Ephron Gausi, a locally based researcher in Malawi who collected data and summarized findings; Liana Fraser, a Canadian-based graduate student who traveled to Uganda to carry out data collection and report writing in Uganda; and to Anne Shileche, a Kenyan Masters student studying in Canada who travelled to Kenya to complete data collection and report writing; Bryn Copp, an MA student in Canada who carried out data collection in Nepal; Adrienne Bolen, a Canadian student who travelled to Guatemala; Tabitha Mirza (co-author on a paper in this collection) who completed research in Tanzania; Somed Shahadu Bitamsimli, PhD student in Canada who carried out research in Ghana (and is author in this collection); Pascale Saint-Denis, an MA student who conducted research in Peru (and is an author in this collection); and Lan Nguyen, a PhD student who conducted research in Vietnam (and is an author in this collection) and Rika Mpogazi, a student in Canada who travelled to Senegal for data collection (and an author in this collection).

Bibliography

Baillie Smith, Matt; Nina, Laurie (2011): International Volunteering and Development: Global Citizenship and Neoliberal Professionalisation Today. In: Transactions of the Institute of British Geographers, vol. 36, no. 4, pp. 545-559.

Baillie Smith, Matt; Nina, Laurie; Griffiths, Mark (2018): South-South Volunteering and Development. In: The Geographical Journal, vol. 184, no. 2, pp. 158-168.

Burns, Danny; Picken, Alexandrea; Hacker, Elisabeth; Aked, Jody; Turner, Katie; Lewis, Simon; Lopez Franco, Erika (2015): The Role of Volunteering in Sustainable Development. https://www.vsointernational.org/sites/default/files/the_role_of_volunteering_in_sustainable_development_2015_vso_ids.pdf (6.8.2021)

Butcher, Jacqueline; Einolf, Christopher (2017): Perspectives on Volunteering: Voices from the South. Geneva.

Campbell Lehn, Carla (2015): Leading Big Volunteer Operations. In: Rosenthal, Robert J. (ed.): Volunteer Engagement 2.0: Ideas and Insights Changing the World. Hoboken, pp. 322-333.

Chen, Li-Ju; Chen, Joseph S. (2011): The Motivations and Expectations of International Volunteer Tourist: A Case Study of "Chinese Village Traditions". In: Tourism Management, vol. 32, no. 2, pp. 435-442.

Clarke, John (2005): Welfare States as Nation States: Some Conceptual Reflections. In: Social Policy and Society, vol. 4, no. 4, pp. 407-415.

Della Porta, Donatella; Andretta, Massimiliano; Mosca, Lorenzo; Reiter, Herbert (2006): Globalization from Below: Transnational Activists and Protest Networks. Minneapolis/ London.

Devereux, Peter (2010): International Volunteers: Cheap Help or Transformational Solidarity Toward Sustainable Development, PhD thesis, Murdoch University. https://researchrepository.murdoch.edu.au/id/eprint/3551/ (6.8.2021).

Devereux, Peter (2008): International Volunteering for Development and Sustainability: Outdated Paternalism or a Radical Response to Globalisation? In: Development in Practice, vol. 18, no. 3, pp. 357-370.

Devereux, Peter; Guse, Kornelia (2012): MDGs, Sustainable Development Goals and the Post 2015 Agenda: Opportunities for Consolidating the Recognition of Volunteerism, https://forum-ids.org/wp-content/uploads/2012/08/2012-Discussion-Paper-Post-2015.pdf (6.8.2021).

Evans, Peter (1996): Introduction: Development Strategies Across the Public-Private Divide. In: World Development, vol. 24, no. 6, pp. 1033-1037.

Fukuda-Parr, Sakiko; Lopes, Carlos; Malik, Khaled (2002): Capacity for Development: New Solutions to Old Problems. London.

Georgeou, Nichole; Engel, Susan (2011): The Impact of Neoliberalism and New Managerialism on Development Volunteering: An Australian Case Study. In: Australian Journal of Political Science, vol. 46, no. 2, pp. 297-311.

GAC – Global Affairs Canada (2017): Canada's Feminist International Assistance Policy. https://www.international.gc.ca/world-monde/assets/pdfs/iap2-eng.pdf?_ga=2.222487771.1927185083.1622431587-1872577644.1613535683 (6.8.2021).

Government of Canada (2020): Canada's Policy for Civil Society Partnerships for International Assistance – A Feminist Approach. https://www.international.gc.ca/world-monde/issues_development-enjeux_developpement/priorities-priorites/civil_policy-politique_civile.aspx?lang=eng (6.8.2021).

Hägel, Peter (2011): Transnational Actors. https://www.oxfordbibliographies.com/view/document/obo-9780199743292/obo-9780199743292-0016.xml (6.8.2021).

Haas, Benjamin; Repenning, Alexander (2018): Transnational knowledge in volunteering for development – A postcolonial approach to weltwärts. In: Transnational Social Review, vol. 8, no. 1, pp. 34-49.

Helms, Sara; McKenzie, Tom (2014): Gender Differences in Formal and Informal Volunteering in Germany. In: Voluntas, vol. 25, no. 4, pp. 887-904.

Heron, Barbara (2007): Desire for Development: Whiteness, Gender, and the Helping Imperative. Waterloo.

Johnson, Tobi (2015): Big Shifts That Will Change Volunteerism for the Better. In: Rosenthal, Robert J. (ed.): Volunteer Engagement 2.0: Ideas and Insights Changing the World. Hoboken, pp. 3-19.

Kanbur, Ravi; Shaffer, Paul (2007): Epistemology, Normative Theory and Poverty Analysis: Implications for Q-Squared in Practice. In: World Development, vol. 35, no. 2, pp. 183-196.

Larsen, Marianne A. (2016): International Service Learning: Engaging Host Communities. New York.

Lee, Young-Joo; Doyeon, Won (2018): Understanding International Volunteering: Who is Most Likely to Participate? In: Journal of Nonprofit and Public Sector Marketing, vol. 30, no. 1, pp. 95-110.

Lewis, David (2006): Globalization and International Service: A Development Perspective. In: Voluntary Action, vol. 7, no. 2, pp. 13-26.

Lindsey, Rose; Mohan, John; Bulloch, Sarah; Metcalfe, Elizabeth (2018): Why People Volunteer: Contextualising Motivation. In: Lindsey, Rose; Mohan, John; Bulloch, Sarah; Metcalfe, Elizabeth (ed.): Continuity and Change in Voluntary Action: Patterns, Trends and Understandings. Bristol/Chicago, pp. 113-152.

Loiseau, Bethina; Sibbald, Rebekah; Raman, Salem A.; Darren, Benedict; Loh, Lawrence C.; Dimaras, Helen (2016): Perceptions of the Role of Short-Term Volunteerism in International Development: Views from Volunteers, Local Hosts, and Community Members. In: Journal of Tropical Medicine, pp. 1-12.

Landolt, Laura K. (2004): (Mis)constructing the Third World? Constructivist analysis of norm diffusion. In: Third World Quarterly, vol. 25, no. 3, pp. 579-591.

Lough, Benjamin J. (2015): The Evolution of International Volunteering. https://www.researchgate.net/publication/282567051_The_Evolution_of_International_Volunteering (6.8.2021).

Lough, Benjamin J. (2014): Social Work Perspectives on International Volunteer Service. In: The British Journal of Social Work, vol. 44, no. 5, pp. 1340-1355.

Lough, Benjamin J.; Tiessen, Rebecca (2018): How do International Volunteering Characteristics Influence Outcomes? Perspectives from Partner Organizations. In: Voluntas, vol. 29, no. 1, pp. 104-118.

Lough, Benjamin J.; Tiessen, Rebecca; Lasker, Judith N. (2018): Effective Practices of International Volunteering for Health: Perspectives from Partner Organizations. In: Globalization and Health, vol. 14, no. 11, pp. 1-11.

Lough, Benjamin J.; Xiang, Xiaoling (2016): Skills-Based International Volunteering Among Older Adults from the United States. In: Administration & Society, vol. 48, no. 9, pp. 1085-1100.

Macdonald, Laura (2018): Canada Goes Global: Building Transnational Relations between Canada and the World, 1968-2017. In: Canadian Foreign Policy Journal, vol. 24, no. 3, pp. 358-371.

Mati, Jacob Mwathi (2017): Models, Developments, and Effects of Transborder Youth Volunteer Exchange Programs in Eastern and Southern Africa. In: Butcher, Jacqueline; Einolf, Christopher (ed.): Perspectives on Volunteering: Voices from the South. Geneva, pp. 129-148.

Mattero, Minna; Campbell-Patton, Charmagne (2008): Measuring the Impact of Youth Voluntary Service Programs: Summary and Conclusions of the International Experts' Meeting. https://www.issuelab.org/resources/3079/3079.pdf (6.8.2021).

Moore McBride, Amanda; Lough, Benjamin J. (2010): Access to International Volunteering. In: Nonprofit Management & Leadership, vol. 21, no. 2, pp. 195-208.

Moser, Caroline (1993): Gender Planning and Development: Theory, Practice and Training. London.

Noxolo, Patricia (2011): Postcolonial Economies of Development Volunteering. In: Pollard, Jane Shelley; McEwan, Cheryl; Hughes, Alex (ed.): Postcolonial Economies. London/New York, pp. 205-228.

Nussbaum, Martha (2003): Capabilities as Fundamental Entitlements: Sen and Social Justice. In: Feminist Economics, vol. 9, no. 2-3, pp. 33-59.

Nye, Joseph; Keohane, Robert O. (1971): Transnational Relations and World Politics: An Introduction. In: International Organization, vol. 25, no. 3, pp. 329-349.

Omoto, Allen; Malsch, Anna; Barraza, Jorge (2009): Compassionate Acts: Motivations for and Correlates of Volunteerism among Older Adults. In: Fehr, Beverley; Sprecher, Susan; Underwood, Lynn (ed.): The Science of Compassionate Love Theory, Research, and Applications. Malden/Oxford, pp. 257-282.

Ostrom, Elinor (1996): Crossing the Great Divide: Coproduction, Synergy, and Development. In: World Development, vol. 24, no. 6, pp. 1073-1087.

Palacios, Carlos M. (2010): Volunteer Tourism, Development and Education in a Postcolonial World: Conceiving Global Connections Beyond Aid. In: Journal of Sustainable Tourism, vol. 18, no. 7, pp. 861-878.

Parpart, Jane L. (2014): Exploring the Transformative Potential of Gender Mainstreaming in International Development Institutions. In: Journal of International Development, vol. 26, no. 3, pp. 382-395.

Perold, Helene; Graham, Lauren A.; Mazembo Mavungu, Eddy; Cronin, Karena; Muchemwa, Learnmore; Lough, Benjamin J. (2013): The Colonial Legacy of International Voluntary Service. In: Community Development Journal, vol. 48, no. 2, pp. 179-196.

Risse, Thomas (2013): Transnational Actors and World Politics. In: Carlsnaes, Walter; Risse, Thomas; Simmons, Beth A. (ed.): Handbook of International Relations. London, pp. 426-451.

Roman, Monica; Muresan, Laura-Mihaela; Manafi, Ioana; Marinescu, Daniela (2018): Volunteering as International Mobility: Recent Evidence from a Post-Socialist Country. In: Transnational Social Review, vol. 8, no. 3, pp. 258-272.

Saffari, Siavash (2016): Can the Subaltern be Heard?: Knowledge Production, Representation, and Responsibility in International Development. In: Transcience Journal, vol. 7, no. 1, pp. 36-46.

Schech, Susanne; Mundkur, Anuradha; Skelton, Tracey; Kothari, Uma (2015): New Spaces of Development Partnership: Rethinking International Volunteering. In: Progress in Development Studies, vol. 15, no. 4, pp. 358-370.

Shriwise, Amanda (2020): Advancing Transnational Approaches to Social Protection in the Global South. In: Schmitt, Carina (ed.): From Colonialism to International Aid: External Actors and Social Protection in the Global South. Switzerland, pp. 19-42.

Smith, Peter (2014): International Volunteer Tourism as (De)commodified Moral Consumption. In: Mostafanezhad, Mary; Hannam, Kevin (ed.): Moral Encounters in Tourism. London, pp. 31-45.

Spivak, Gayatri Chakravorty (1999): A Critique of Postcolonial Reason: Toward a History of the Vanishing Present. Cambridge/London.

Tiessen, Rebecca (2018): Learning and Volunteering Abroad for Development: Unpacking Host Organisation and Volunteer Rationales. Abingdon/New York.

Tiessen, Rebecca (2015): Gender Essentialism in Canadian Foreign Aid Commitments to Women, Peace, and Security. In: International Journal, vol. 70, no. 1, pp. 84-100.

Tiessen, Rebecca; Baranyi, Stephen (2017): Obligations and Omissions: Canada's Ambiguous Actions on Gender Equality. Montreal.

Tiessen, Rebecca; Lough, Benjamin J.; Cheung, Samuel (2018): Introduction: A Theoretical and Methodological Case for Examining Agency and Power Relations North-South Volunteering Research Collaborations. In: Tiessen, Rebecca; Lough, Benjamin J.; Grantham, Kate (ed.): Insights on International Volunteering. Perspectives From the Global South. Germany, pp. 7-20.

Tiessen, Rebecca; Paritosh, Kumar (2013): Ethical Challenges Encountered on Learning/Volunteer Abroad Programmes for Students in International Development Studies in Canada: Youth Perspectives and Educator Insights. In: Canadian Journal of Development Studies / Revue canadienne d'études du développement, vol. 34, no. 3, pp. 416-430.

Tiessen, Rebecca; Rao, Sheila; Lough, Benjamin J. (2021): International Volunteering as Transformational Feminist Practice for Gender Equality. In: Journal of Developing Societies, vol. 37, no. 1, pp. 30-56.

Tiessen, Rebecca; Swan, Emma (2018): Canada's Feminist Foreign Policy Promises: An Ambitious Agenda for Gender Equality, Human Rights, Peace, and Security. in: Hill, Norman; Lagassé, Philippe (ed.): Justin Trudeau and Canadian Foreign Policy. New York, pp. 187-205.

Trau, Adam M. (2015): Challenges and Dilemmas of International Development Volunteering: A Case Study from Vanuatu. In: Development in Practice, vol. 25, no. 1, pp. 29-41.

United Nations (2016): Gender Equality 'Greatest Human Rights Challenge of Our Time', Secretary-General Tells High-Level Panel on Women's Economic Empowerment. https://www.un.org/press/en/2016/sgsm18122.doc.htm (6.8.2021).

United Nations Volunteers (2017): Volunteer Solutions for Poverty Reduction and Economic Empowerment of Women and Youth. https://www.unv.org/success-stories/Volunteer-solutions-poverty-reduction-and-economic-empowerment-women-and-youth (6.8.2021).

Zwingel, Susanne (2012): How Do Norms Travel? Theorizing International Women's Rights in Transnational Perspective. In: International Studies Quarterly, vol. 56, no. 1, pp. 115-129.

ARTICLES

Capacity Building and Capability Development: Understanding the Relations of Power and Exchange Between International Development Volunteers and Partner Organizations and Communities

Khursheed Sadat

1. Introduction

The contributions of international development volunteers (IDVs) to the capacity development of partner organizations and communities has been well documented (Lough et al. 2011; Aked 2015; Lough/Oppenheim 2017; Nyirenda 2018; McLachlan/Binns 2019). Underexplored are the nature of these relationships, particularly as it concerns the relations of power within these exchanges between IDVs and partners, and their impacts on the process of capacity building. This paper fills this deficit by engaging in an analysis of the dynamics of power between these two parties and the ways in which it impacts the processes of capacity building of partner organizations and communities, bringing nuance to these discussions. In this paper, I draw upon the data from our study to confirm that IDVs contribute to the capacity building of partner organizations and communities through skills and capability development as well as being employed as resources. Furthermore, I argue that the relations of interaction and exchange between these two parties are constituted by complex and dynamic power relations in which both parties collaboratively shape how the capacity of organizations and communities are developed.

I begin the paper with a brief discussion of the capabilities approach as the theoretical lens around which this paper is framed. I follow this with a discussion of relevant scholarship, illustrating gaps in knowledge and situating this paper within it. Third, I include a detailed account of the findings as they relate to impacts of the engagements between IDVs and partner organizations on the process of capacity building. Finally, I analyze the findings of this research, deconstructing the ways in which interactions and partnerships between IDVs and partners shape the capacity building process.

2. Theoretical Framework and Literature Review

The arguments and evidence of this paper are framed by the theoretical lens of the capabilities approach. Introduced by Sen (1999), this approach identifies development as constituting of building peoples' capability, which entails providing people opportunities and freedoms, particularly through access to healthcare and education, in order for them to be able to choose how to live (Sen 1999; Nussbaum 2011). Sen (1999) argues that this approach is agent-oriented as policies and practices of development are there to support people to shape their own lives and futures. Nussbaum (2011) makes the distinction between internal capabilities, trained or developed personal traits, and combined capabilities, the environment surrounding individuals that allows them to express their internal capabilities. In this paper I examine the influence of partnerships between IDVs and partner organizations on both types of capabilities. Specifically, in this paper I employ Nussbaum's adaptation of Sen's capabilities approach, which makes a conscious and explicit objective to address issues of gender inequality and injustice, as the main arguments and evidence on the process of capacity building center around power relations.

In line with the capabilities approach, I define capacity building of partner organizations and communities using the Organization for Economic Co-operation and Development (OECD) definition which refers to the central role of enabling environments in cultivating opportunities and freedoms for the growth and change of individuals and organizations (OECD 2011).

2.1 Literature Review

There is a wealth of literature examining the contributions of IDVs to the capacity building of host organizations (Lough et al. 2011; Nyirenda 2018; McLachlan/Binns 2019). These contributions of IDVs consist of building organizational capacity through providing training to develop skills, such as in areas of documentation, computing and organizational management (McLachlan/Binns 2019; Nyrienda 2018). Research shows that IDVs have utilized their technical and professional skills to serve as resources to organizations, or serve as extra hands, a task accessible for even unskilled IDVs (Lough et al. 2011). Also, studies have revealed that IDVs have provided resources such as money and supplies, and even their own social capital to help sustain partner organizations (Lough et al. 2011). Furthermore, IDVs are found to enrich the intercultural competence of organizational staff through sharing knowledge and experiences (Lough et al. 2011). This body of literature on the contributions of IDVs to capacity building of partner organizations and communities generally situates these partners as recipients of services and resources, overlooking the practices of knowledge and skills transfer to the capability development of these partners, particularly as it relates to their expressions of agency in the process of building capacity, revealing scope for further research.

Furthermore, these analyses of IDV contributions largely center on the instrumental value of these volunteers, necessitating discussions of the relationship of deep-rooted structural issues, particularly gender inequality, to the process of capacity building, and whether and in what ways they are addressed in engagements between IDVs and partners.

In addition to highlighting the contributions of IDVs to the capacity building of partner organizations and communities, the literature also identifies several factors that pose challenges for IDV in this endeavor. The factors that mitigate the contributions of IDVs to capacity building include issues with language and communication, problematic attitudes of IDVs, issues of adaptation, issues of placement incompatibility as well as duration of service (Lough et al. 2011; McLachlan/Binns 2019; Nyirenda 2018; Tiessen/Lough 2018). The salient theme drawn from this list of mitigating factors is deficiencies in communication between hosts and IDVs, which suggests the need to further explore opportunities to enhance communication and nurture relationship-building.

Reflecting on the concept of relationality and its relevance to capacity building of host organizations, Lough et al. (2011) note that relationships between IDVs and organizational staff have the potential to be constituted by asymmetrical power relations, as the positionality of IDVs – who largely originate from "developed nations" – privileges their voice over local voices, which may result in the devaluation of local knowledge and cultures, an issue discussed in other scholarship (Perold et al. 2013; Hawkes 2014; Lough/Oppenheim 2017). This poses a challenge to capacity building as valuing local knowledge and skills are integral to the volunteer placements (Girgis 2007; Mclachlan/Binns 2019). The problematic role of outsider development actors who act as 'experts' on development issues in partner countries has been extensively covered in the development literature, with examples of superiority complexes and lack of mutual learning (Parpart 1995; Kothari 2005; Girgis 2007; Ferguson 2015). These studies provide scope for research on the relationships between/across IDVs, partner organizations, and communities in order to explore the potential for problematic and/or mutually beneficial relations of exchange and capacity building opportunities.

Development scholarship has explored the relevance of the quality of relationships between IDVs and host organizations as it relates to capacity building outcomes (Hawke 2014; Tiessen/Lough 2018; Mclachlan/Binns 2019). For instance, in a study of the factors that shape the contribution of IDVs to capacity building, Hawkes (2014) finds that the quality of the relationships between IDVs and hosts is an influential variable. Tiessen and Lough's (2018) research corroborates these findings, revealing that organizational staff perceive "team-oriented training" between IDVs and themselves as integral to practices of skills transfer, connecting it to experiences of greater ownership and sustainability of organizational capacity. Girgis (2007) witnesses that relationships of exchange between international development actors and local communities are successful at building capacity when development actors inquire into, respect and value local knowledge and skills, thus, characterizing partnership.

Relatedly, Impey and Overton (2013) argue that relationships based on partnerships are founded on reciprocity and respect. Aked (2015) expands on this idea and finds that partnerships are cultivated through informal practices in which parties connect on a personal level. Regarding reciprocity, Lough and Oppenheim's (2017) research offers insight into the multiple forms of reciprocal relationships between IDVs and hosts, documenting how these relationships are practiced, and the variables that shape the impact of these mutual relationships. These studies speak to the role of reciprocity in capacity building strategies, but offer limited details about the nature of the relationships, including the nuances of their dynamics, negotiation of power relations, strategies employed and opportunities for asserting agency among organizational staff and communities.

The findings analyzed in this paper offer insights into the distinctive contributions IDVs make through the process of relationship-building with partner organizations, highlighting the power dynamics of transnational relationships and opportunities for negotiation, mutual learning and reciprocal exchange.

3. Methods

Interviews were conducted in 2018 – 2019 with 150 partner organization staff in ten countries. Once all interviews were transcribed, data were coded to identify common themes throughout. Data were analyzed using discourse analysis. The introduction to this special edition has more detailed information on the methodology for data collection and the analysis of findings.

4. Findings

Findings from these data highlight many references to diverse strategies for capacity building and the impacts on capability development resulting from IDVs working in partnership with organizations around the world. The findings highlight several themes as they relate to capacity building, including knowledge and skills transfer; capability development; bridging the cultural divide; and IDVs as a vital resource for improving inclusion and participation. The data demonstrate the significance of partnerships, reciprocity, and relationship building as factors that shape the outcomes of IDV engagement with partner organizations and communities. In this section, I share the experiences of partner organizations who commented on their experiences working with IDVs and their insights regarding the impact of IDVs in relationship to capability development and capacity building.

4.1 Knowledge and Skills Transfer

The findings reveal that international volunteers play an important role in bridging knowledge gaps of partner organizations and communities with regards to the process of capacity building. IDVs combine their expertise with intensive interactions with partner organization staff throughout their volunteer service and in so doing, also enhance their own capacities and skills-building through mutual learning in these transnational interactions.

Despite the two-way learning that is highly regarded as a major contribution of IDVs, there were many references to the nature of the skills and competencies that IDVs bring to partner organizations. Some of these skills included technical contributions such as creating and maintaining websites as well as online marketing and operating social media. The technical skills of documentation, which entails the specific procedure on how to write documents, particularly project reports, budget reports, as well as emails, were all identified across the research sites as necessary and valuable skills in operating the partner organizations. For instance, detailing the role of IDVs, one participant from Tanzania stated, "We do all things with her: documenting, analyzing, proposal [writing]; but also preparing the budget for the proposal." This participant illustrates the invaluable role IDVs play in supporting the partner organizational staff in operations of these partner organizations.

Other skills transferred through IDVs included time management, language and interpersonal skills. Particularly, the transfer of IDV language skills was reported by hosts as highly successful. For instance, one Nepalese staff member revealed, "I cannot speak proper English, but when volunteers are here I am responsible to communicate with them, so while communicating with them my English-speaking capacity had improved." Similarly, several partner organization staff members noted that their facility in English language improved as a result of IDV contributions.

The transfer of business management and entrepreneurial skills to host organizations and beneficiaries of the partner organizations was recognized as a salient outcome from IDV engagement with host organizations. For instance, the data on Malawi demonstrate that women were trained in dairy farming, which included tools and education on how to produce profit from such work. A participant from Ghana stated that through transferring entrepreneurial skills, IDVs supported the strengthening of women's economic voice, where farmers are equipped with the capability "to sell their produce and also negotiate for good prices." IDV support for women's economic voice was also evidenced in the data from Senegal, Uganda, Malawi, Guatemala and Tanzania, revealing that the transference of knowledge and skills on financial literacy and business development served to support women to become economically independent.

The findings show that IDVs worked to strengthen analytical skills and helped develop these through engagement with hosts. For example, a participant from Tanzania speaking about the experience with an IDV reported how the IDV helped organization staff engage in critical analysis before making decisions and encouraged staff to look more deeply at the root causes of a problem. The IDV's contributions were considered highly valuable to the team, providing support to "be more analytical and unpack every kind of discussion which you have or any event which you encounter", which can help organization staff move beyond the symptoms of a problem and better understand the underlying reasons for development challenges. These critical analytical skills encouraged by IDVs were particularly important in relation to gender equality and women's empowerment (GEWE) work. As one study participant from Malawi noted: "I think we value what they have brought to the organization and contributions they make for us to have a better understanding on issues of gender and women empowerment. I think it's very beneficial."

4.2 Capability Development and Bridging the Cultural Divide

The findings demonstrate that the transfer of situated cultural knowledge occurs through intercultural communication, which takes place through interactions between IDVs and hosts. For instance, the data from both Malawi and Vietnam reveal that cultural knowledge on Western working styles are shared, such as strict deadlines and clear boundaries between work and breaks, and when adopted they serve to promote efficiency within host organizations.

The findings reveal that cultural interactions between hosts and IDVs from diverse backgrounds work to promote diversity and the cultivation of intercultural and interpersonal skills. For example, a staff member of a partner organization in Peru reflecting on the diverse background of IDVs stated, "The fact that some of those people were immigrants [to Canada] has been very useful for us...because they bring different cultures and knowledge of the region that brings us a lot." This staff member recognizes the diverse backgrounds of Canadian IDVs as beneficial for their organization as they are gaining knowledge of the diverse cultures and experiences.

In relation to knowledge sharing related to GEWE, participants from Vietnam, Uganda and Peru highlighted the value of conversations between IDVs and hosts, including discussions on cultural differences in gender roles as important for shaping views and understandings of their own countries. For example, reflecting on their interactions with IDVs, a participant from Peru stated:

> *I like to converse about those things with them, because their culture has made*
> *it so they have more information on gender equality, and not only that they*
> *have more information, but they have been able to practice it and insert it in*

their lives and bring it to this country. It's great to be able to learn from them, so they don't only come to support us but they also teach us a lot on that theme. They have taught me a lot on feminism and equal opportunities.

This participant values the culturally specific knowledge on gender the IDV brought to their work, expressing how IDVs' knowledge shapes their daily practices as informed by feminism.

The findings from Kenya reveal that sharing situated cultural and experiential knowledge between IDVs and hosts introduces alternative realities, particularly to members of host communities, wherein their knowledge of the world expands as does their hope for their future opportunities. The findings from Senegal expand on this, identifying that both IDVs and hosts have their own knowledge and realities which do not always align. However, the interaction between the IDVs and partners facilitates the process of hybridization of knowledge and practices. A participant from Senegal asserts:

Well, now, it is best to take into account the values of one's own community and that of someone else and maybe, that is what allows us to formulate a new reality. That's how I see things but I don't think that certain things can directly influence what happens here.

This participant suggests that the residual effect of these interactions between IDVs and partners are gradual changes in organizational and community practices. In turn, these interactions with IDVs create opportunities to consider when and if change is needed to correct practices that are not working in the capacity building process for marginalized/oppressed people.

4.3   Building Capabilities of IDVs

Partner organization staff also provided a number of examples of ways that capacity building was carried out with the IDVs, highlighting the nature of exchange of knowledge and skill-sharing. For example, partner organizations identified the need to equip IDVs with knowledge of the context in which they are working in. For instance, one participant from Malawi suggested for IDVs "[t]o have a little bit understanding of where we are as a country at the moment, maybe to better understand the challenge that they will meet as we implement the project of gender [and] women['s] empowerment." Adding to this, a participant from Guatemala reinforced the importance of IDVs understanding "the local dynamics of the country where they are going to be, and to understand the cultural history and the limits that women have." Other important learning opportunities for IDVs included improved understanding of group dynamics and the nature of gender relations within the Guatemalan context, which are very specific to the cultural norms and practices of the country. The responsibility and ownership of partner organization staff for their organizations and communities is communicated in these sugges-tions and recommendations they provide IDVs, informing them what is required of them in their placement in order to work effectively. These examples highlight the contribution partner organizations make to expanding the knowledge of IDVs beyond the abstract or theoretical ideas they may bring with them. These exchanges between IDVs and partner organizations demonstrate the ways in which reciproc-ity and partnership are fundamental to the capacity building process.

4.4 IDV as a Resource for Improved Inclusion and Participation

The findings show that IDVs serve as resources in supporting inclusive participa-tion and policy making with partner organizations and communities, a role that is highly valued by partner organization staff. Examples from partner organization staff in Peru, Uganda, Ghana, Malawi and Tanzania included their appreciation for the dedicated efforts of IDVs to champion gender equality as central to all work. IDVs engaged in a number of strategies to ensure a strong focus on gender equal-ity including introducing a gender focus in the programs they operated; calling for increased participation of women in all activities to ensure equal representation; and supporting partner staff with the knowledge and tools to succeed in their roles. One example from Ghana highlights the championing role of IDVs in the training of broadcasters in gender and media. As one participant noted, IDVs:

Help to develop materials for the broadcasters, and also assist them with prac-tical modules for gender inclusion in the local media. We had one that helped us to design a monitoring tool for capturing or measuring gender inclusion in our radio programming, and that was very fantastic (Ghana).

Moreover, in Malawi, IDVs advocated for increased participation of mothers in the workplace, working with host organizations to create a private space so working mothers can nurse their children at work, thus addressing the issue of equal partic-ipation in the public sphere.

For partner organization staff in Ghana, IDVs were identified as individuals who had a voice in issues of gender equality and were more likely to be heard than local staff when championing gender equality. The knowledge and experience that IDVs have with topics related to gender equality were welcomed by many who saw IDVs as better able to introduce new ideas. As one Ghanaian counterpart noted, IDVs have "distinctly impacted" their work, offering support in areas that can be off lim-its for some Ghanaians to address – "no-go" topics. The counterpart went on to say,

What I think they [international volunteers] have distinctly impacted is, you know our Ghanaian culture and the way some of these gender issues is a no-go area. I think it is easier for people to hear and accept it when it is coming from someone that is not a part of you. When you are a woman in our community, and you are talking about gender equality you look very strange to your male counterparts. But somebody from another culture bringing that helps (Ghana).

However, the findings from Uganda illustrate that sometimes the knowledge and voices of IDVs can be disregarded as irrelevant to the local context or seen as introducing foreign ideas that are not seen as applicable in the country. As a Ugandan study participant summarized,

Normally there are cultural issues within our society in terms of gender equality. I've seen international volunteers come up to speak about issues that people don't seem to consider of such importance. Often, this isn't taken very well and I don't think it's caused any issues within the organization.

Despite the reservations highlighted by this partner organization staff member, the study participant concluded the statement by indicating an appreciation for the contributions of IDVs, saying "I value their opinions", demonstrating the ambivalence and complexity surrounding the value of IDV contributions.

The findings from this study demonstrate that IDVs use their expertise to directly contribute to the operations of partner organizations. For instance, a participant from Uganda described the role of IDVs as supporting "our communications department in terms of developing articles, and especially updating our websites and updating our social media platforms." Adding to this, the data from Senegal reveals that IDVs help institutionalize partner organization efforts to improve the living conditions and political representation of Senegalese women by reaching out to women's groups, female politicians and community leaders by working to organize their pre-existing work structures and prepare official documents that could be presented to local political authorities and institutions. Thus, IDVs employ their skills with management, advocacy, documentation and social media to aid in the operations of organizations and support their work with international partners.

IDVs are valued for their contributions to communication and networking, such as facilitating communication between organizations and donors, development organizations, other local institutions, and the local communities. Examples of the interlocuter roles of IDVs were noted by participants in Malawi, Tanzania, Senegal, Uganda, Ghana, and Kenya. As the counterpart from Malawi noted, IDVs play an important role "as liaison person between us and the United Nations (UN), not UN as a whole but the United Nations Development Programme (UNDP)." Adding to this, the Malawian counterpart noted that the IDV is able to represent the organization in meetings.

A counterpart from Tanzania highlighted the important role of IDVs in facilitating networking and communications by working with ambassadors from different countries, building important connections to different ambassadors. In witnessing this contribution of IDVs, this Tanzanian participant went on to state, "now we are connected, because those offices now are calling, she's not here, but they are calling back." The impact of this networking role continues to be felt after the volunteer left and was considered essential for making their organization more visible and known to others – even more trusted within the community.

The study findings also provided insight into the valued services IDVs brought to gender equality work. As one study participant from Peru noted, the IDV brought expertise and experience that was "fundamental" to the team. The counterpart from Peru goes on to explain that the IDVs play an important role in the early stages of the gender network in Peru. The counterpart appreciated the diversity of professional IDVs that her organization worked with. One of the IDVs she worked with was a psychologist who "provided us with a different point of view to attend to the problems of violence against women or to analyze the situation of violence against women." The Peruvian counterpart concludes that the contributions of the IDVs were crucial to the success of the gender network. The expert skills of the IDV in this case were identified as fundamental to the operation of the organization.

4.5 Factors That Facilitate the Collaborative Process

At the heart of the contributions of IDVs to partner organizations and communities are a set of distinctive contributions and characteristics of the value addition of IDVs. Partner organizations explained these distinctive contributions as acts of reciprocity and dedicated partnerships cultivated through a commitment to relationship building.

Interactions between IDVs and partners are marked by the practice of reciprocity in which the knowledge and understanding of both sides are developed (Tanzania; Vietnam; Uganda; Malawi). For instance, a participant from Uganda explains:

Most of the volunteers, [...] before they go, we ask them to share their cultural backgrounds like: What happens in your culture?; How are women treated?; What are some of the gender roles that women are supposed to respect in their country? And then we have people here share what is happening in their communities. So when they share about ideas, they both learn from each other. The volunteers learn from the young girls here and they learn a lot from the volunteers.

Adding to this, a participant from Malawi said that they have learned so many things as a result of working with international volunteers but at the same time the Malawian partners "also equip them as well with how we do it here. So it's an exchange of experiences and innovative ideas."

As the evidence demonstrates, the capacities of both parties are developed through interaction, constituting it as a collaborative engagement.

Similarly, experiences of partnership are observed when working with IDVs. One participant from Tanzania describes the partnership experience as working together, taking time to sit together and share what each considers is important for women. From these conversations, agreements on a way forward for supporting women is achieved, and a strategic plan is put in place for how to better reach women in their project activities and through trainings. The partnership is considered highly valuable in this case because it is a commitment to the exchange of ideas that shapes the next steps for completing the work. As partners in the co-design of strategies to address GEWE, both the partner organization and the IDV bring something to the table. It is their combined efforts and exchange of knowledge that is seen to advance the organization's work.

Another partner from Tanzania remarks that working with volunteers is beneficial because it adds value to the organization's existing work. Working alone can be challenging and the partnership model between partner organization staff and IDVs is generative, bringing up new and different ideas collectively. The process of bringing together individual views and ideas "contributes something as a whole, something new" (Tanzania). Thus, working in partnership allows for cultivating innovative solutions to issues, as occurs through the dialectical engagement between different parties who pool their intellectual and experiential resources.

Facilitating this collaborative process is the practice of building relationships. The findings illustrate that there are many factors that facilitate the process of relationship building between IDVs and partner organization staff. For example, a participant from Tanzania describes the nature of relationship building and the ways that this happens. For the Tanzanian counterpart, relationship building happens when "we sit together during lunch, we make friends, we talk. ... It's the chance we have to interact and share." As this testimony reveals, the practice of congregating in informal spaces to share experiences and knowledge, serves to cultivate friendships between IDVs and hosts. Similarly, the data on Senegal reveals that IDV live and work with the locals to cultivate connections and build relationships.

Reflecting on the value of relationships for knowledge and skills development, a participant from Guatemala states,

> *I think I value how she is as a person the most. Because listen, I could find someone with the best professional skills, but if we didn't connect at the personal level, then we wouldn't be able to accomplish the same things. So, this is how it is so much better that we have a close relationship.*

This final quote offers rich insights into the distinctive contributions that IDV programs make to relationship building and the nature of a reciprocal capacity building model. While capacity building research in IDV programs has largely focused on the transfer of skills or nature of competency building dynamics, these findings highlight the qualitative nature of how and when relationship building happens. These findings speak to the importance of building trust, mutual respect and friendship as characteristics of the partnerships that emerge between IDVs and organization staff in the Global South.

5. Analysis

The examples provided by partner organization staff of the role and contributions of IDVs to gender equality programming, skills development, and capacity building expands our understanding of the value accorded to IDVs by host organizations.

Beyond developing individual skills and general competencies, the findings summarized here demonstrate the nature of how relationships are formed in addition to sharing knowledge and skills. Together, these factors contribute to capability development for both the partner organization staff and the IDVs. The transfer of skills and knowledge between IDVs and partner organization staff and communities was found to be connected to experiences of agency and enhanced independence of partner organization staff. For example, the findings highlight how women in host communities worked with IDVs to gain knowledge of farming practice, as well as through training on business management and entrepreneurship. These services translated into new opportunities for women to generate an income and to advance their social and economic standing in their communities. Equipped with the skills and tools to manage themselves productively and independently, women were able to sell their produce and actively engage in determining the price of their products.

The development of individual capabilities noted in these examples and as defined by Sen's (1999) analytical lens, serves to expand people's freedoms. Capability development is recognized to take place particularly through practices of education, which aim to facilitate peoples increased participation in social, political and economic systems of their communities and beyond (Sen 1999). Previous studies exploring the relationship between gender and microfinance have discussed that participating in the public sphere and having entrepreneurial skills is not in itself empowering. The literature reveals a tension between a subject's agency and the structures of power surrounding them, namely patriarchy and capitalism, that limit agency (Roberts/Soederberg 2012; Wilson 2015).

The findings in this research project demonstrate that in addition to aiding the development of technical skills, IDVs engaged in the transfer of analytical skills with partner organizations and communities. Partners applied these analytical skills to theorize on the source and nature of the social, political and economic issues they are facing. For instance, as the findings from Tanzania reveal, discussions between both parties constituted a deeper inquiry into the root causes of issues serving to equip partner organizations with the tools to address problems and take a transformative approach, rather than simply addressing the symptoms of problems. Furthermore, the evidence from Malawi illustrates that through the practices of developing their analytical skills, partner organization staff reported that they were engaging in discussions of issues of gender inequality and women's empowerment with IDVs and found those experiences to have developed their understanding of these topics. These exchanges and discussions between IDVs and partner organizations and communities serve to build the capabilities of all parties involved, building their skill set while also transforming the environments in which they live and work. These exchanges are valued for addressing the structures that mitigate individual agency by constructing enabling environments that allow participants to be able to build their own capacities.

Attempts to address the source and nature of social, political and economic issues are evidenced to have also taken place through intercultural interactions which include discussions of lived experience between IDVs and partners. The findings reveal that both parties engaged in discussions of cultural traditions, practices and gender norms. McLachlan and Binns (2019) argue that cross-cultural exchanges constituted by relations of reciprocity serve to mitigate unequal power relations between IDVs and host communities as they both value the knowledge and experiences they share. Centering their analysis of the impacts of intercultural exchanges on the power dynamics between IDVs and host communities, these scholars leave unexplored a discussion of the impacts of the content of these exchanges on capability development (McLachlan/Binns 2019).

This study has demonstrated that sharing cultural knowledge provides partners with innovative tools to address problems and build for their future. For instance, in the data from Peru, IDV's culturally specific knowledge on the issue of gender inequality, and how it is addressed in their home communities, is recognized as valuable by the staff of partner organizations; partner organization staff expressed their intent on applying these approaches to the context in which they live in order to destabilize unequal power relations. However, the data from Senegal reveals that host communities do not just replace their own approaches with that of IDVs, rather in these cultural transactions, hosts maintain their own knowledge and tools, and add the experiences, knowledge and unique insights of IDVs to their own collection to generate new tools and "formulate new realities". These findings provide insights into the synergistic impact of collaborative models between IDVs and partner organizations.

Adding to the synergistic benefits of collaboration, findings from Kenya show that intercultural interactions result in the expansion of the partner community's worldview and aid in the cultivation of hope for the future. The expansion of worldviews is also experienced by the IDVs who gain valuable culturally-specific information as a result of their interactions with partner organizations and communities. The transfer of cultural knowledge builds the capabilities of IDVs and partner organizations by equipping both with the knowledge and tools to address issues of inequality in the spaces in which they live and work. These exchanges also expand the worldviews of IDVs and partner organizations, inspiring both to dream of their future and themselves, aiding in the cultivations of spaces in which they can express their agency.

Cross-cultural exchanges between IDVs and partners provide rich opportunities for reciprocal learning and knowledge sharing. The evidence in this research echoes that of Lough and Oppenheim (2017) who find that relations of cultural exchange are reciprocal in nature and thus beneficial to both. In the exchanges of knowledge and experiences, IDVs become informed of cultural practices, particularly surrounding gender roles and norms through conversations with organizational staff and members of the community. Partner organization staff play a pivotal role in shaping the knowledge and understanding of IDVs by helping them develop their knowledge of the context, culture, history, and interpersonal and inter-institutional relationships. To further enhance the opportunities for expanded learning among IDVs, partner organizations suggested that IDVs spend more time at the start of their mandates developing an understanding of the nature of power relations in the spaces in which they are working.

Greater attention to improved training and orientation of IDVs to local cultural realities is believed to be a strategy that will better equip IDVs to be effective when addressing issues in the local contexts and enhance their performance throughout their mandates. This recommendation is supported by the research of Mclachlan and Binns (2019) who observe that the knowledge extracted from partner communities on values, traditions, and practices are essential in delivering successful grassroots development projects. The power and agency of hosts is expressed in the exchanges with IDVs as they aid in building the capabilities of IDVs by first identifying their knowledge and skill gaps and then curating the knowledge and tools for these volunteers to better steer the direction of their own capacity development.

Among the most significant contributions made by IDVs, networking and bridging relationships was seen as highly valuable. IDVs played an important role as liaisons between partner organizations and other development agencies, funders and institutions which were seen as constructive and valuable to the operations of partner organizations. Yet, this contribution must be considered in relation to the structural challenges that prevail. Persistent power imbalances between the Global North and Global South continue to privilege the voices of IDVs over local staff, thus perpetuating unequal relations (Perold et al. 2013; Lough/Oppenheim 2017). However, an analysis of the perspectives of partner organizations and communities on these relations of exchange brings nuance to these discussions. For instance, hosts reported that IDVs have a voice when they introduce topics and discuss "controversial" or foreign ideas with local staff. Their position as foreigners privileges their knowledge and voice with understanding and respect from the local staff, local agencies, and institutions. This gives IDVs an avenue to champion the priorities of the partner organization staff. Also, IDVs were able to use their privilege to call for the increased participation of women, and in advocating for equal participation of women in activities, as well as aiding in the inclusive policy making of partner organizations (Aked 2015). Thus, IDVs are seen by partner organization staff as a way to begin to deconstruct unequal power relations.

The power of host organizations and communities is not only cultivated through these relations of exchange with IDVs, it also exists and is expressed prior to and during these exchanges. The findings demonstrate that the partner organizations express their power through sharing their perspectives on what type of relationship has worked for them in building their capacity, the ways in which it has worked, as well as detailing how these relationships are cultivated, thus indirectly determining the terms of their relationship. For example, the data from Tanzania reveals that partnerships between IDVs and host organization staff are valued as they are constituted by collaborative practices in which both parties contribute equally, value each other's perspectives, and come to mutual understandings and unanimous decisions. The data illustrates that host organization staff value their own power and recognize that both parties bring valuable knowledge and skills to the table. Thus, in communicating their perspectives and preferences, partners are actively defining the terms of these relationships.

6. Conclusion

Through the lens of capabilities development, this paper examined the nature of transnational exchanges between IDVs and partner organization staff and communities in relation to capacity building. In this paper, capabilities development refers to the process of cultivating an environment in which people have the opportunities and freedoms to choose how to live (Sen 1999). With respect to the capacity building of partner organizations and communities, these partners worked collaboratively with IDVs to develop their capabilities, integral to the process of capacity building. Through the transfer of skills and knowledge, both technical and culturally specific, both IDVs and partner organization staff and communities become equipped with the tools to address the symptoms as well as the root causes of issues, and work towards building their respective capabilities. The combined focus on symptoms and root causes in development work was particularly important to GEWE policymaking and programming. In fact, partner organization staff revealed that gender inclusive policymaking and programming was championed by IDVs, who served as valuable resources to these organizations. Evidenced to have impactful voices in spaces in which partner organization staff and communities do not, IDVs utilize their privilege and take on the role of representing the interests of these staff and communities in matters of capacity building and capability development. However, partner organization staff exercise power in practices of capacity building with IDVs, as they define the terms of the relationships of exchange in sharing their perspective of the nature of relationship to be built and through which mechanisms they deem most effective in building capacity. Partnership and reciprocity, cultivated through a commitment to relationship building characterized the nature of the collaborative capacity building process between IDVs and partner organizations and communities.

Bibliography

Aked, Jody (2015): What's different about how volunteers work? Relationship building for wellbeing and change. In: IDS Bulletin, vol. 46, no. 5, pp. 29–42.

Ferguson, Lucy (2015): This is our gender person. The messy business of working as a gender expert in international development. In: International Feminist Journal of Politics, vol. 17, no.3, pp. 380-397.

Girgis, Mona (2007): The capacity building paradox. Using friendship to build capacity in the South. In: Development in Practice, vol. 17, no. 3, pp. 353-366.

Hawkes, Martine (2014): International volunteerism. Supports and barriers to capacity development outcomes. In: Third Sector Review, vol. 20, No. 1, pp. 1-11.

Impey, Kathy; Overton, John (2013): Developing Partnerships. The Assertion of Local Control of International Development Volunteers in South Africa. In: Community Development Journal, vol. 49, No. 1, pp. 111-128.

Kothari, Uma (2005): Authority and Expertise. The Professionalization Of International Development And The Ordering Of Dissent. In: Antipode, pp. 425-446.

Lough, Benjamin J.; Moore-McBridge, Amanda; Sherraden, Margaret S.; O'Hara, Kathleen (2011): Capacity building contributions of short-term international volunteers. In: Journal of Community Practice, vol. 19, pp. 120-137.

Lough, Benjamin J.; Oppenheim, Willy (2017): revisiting reciprocity in international volunteering. In: Progress in Development Studies, vol. 17, no. 3, pp. 197-213.

McLachlan, Sam; Binns, Tony (2019): Exploring Host Perspectives Towards Younger International Development Volunteers. In: Development in Practice, vol. 29, no. 1, pp. 65-79.

Nussbaum, Martha (2011): Creating Capabilities. The Human Development Approach. Cambridge.

Nyirenda, Denis (2018): Malawi: Mixed Results Form International Volunteers in Organizational Development and Capacity Building. In: Tiessen, Rebecca; Lough, Benjamin J.;

Grantham, Kate (ed.): Insights on International Volunteering. Perspectives From the Global South. Germany, pp. 87-97.

OECD (2011): The enabling environment for capacity development. https://www.oecd.org/ dac/accountable-effective-institutions/48315248.pdf (30.6.2021).

Parpart, Jane L. (1995): Chapter 12: deconstructing the development expert: gender, development and the vulnerable. In: Marchand, Marianne H.; Parpart, Jane L. (ed.): Feminism/ Postmodernism/Development. London, pp. 221-243.

Perold, Helena; Graham, Lauren A.; Mazembo Mavungu, Eddy; Cronin, Karena; Muchemwa, Learnmore; Lough, Bejamin (2013): The colonial legacy of international voluntary service. In: Community Development Journal, vol. 48, pp. 179–96.

Roberts, Adrienne; Soederberg, Susanne (2012): Gender equality as smart economics? A critique of the 2012 World Development Report. In: Third World Quarterly, vol. 33, no. 5, pp. 949-968.

Sen, Amartya (1999): Development as Freedom. New York.

Tiessen, Rebecca; Lough J., Benjamin (2018): International volunteering capacity development. Volunteer partner organization experiences of mitigating factors for effective practice. In: Forum for Development Studies, pp. 1-21.

Wilson, Kalpana (2015): Towards a radical re-appropriation: gender, development and neoliberal feminism. In: Development and Change, vol. 46, no. 4, pp. 803-832.

Creating Cosmopolitan Identities in Transnational Spaces to Advance Gender Equality

Leva Rouhani

1. Introduction

The unprecedented rise of international development volunteering (IDV) over the past few decades has corresponded with the rise in research around the impact of IDVs making a distinctive contribution to the broader landscape of development work and the implications of understanding IDVs as transnational actors. Central to this analysis is understanding the distinctive role the relationships and partnerships between IDVs and receiving organizations play in creating transnational spaces where dialogue and the diffusion of norms around gender equality programming has created new cosmopolitan identities.

This paper will analyze how IDVs use transnational spaces to build relational networks among partner organizations that support gender equality outcomes. Specifically, this paper will explore how cosmopolitan identities of partner organizations are shaped by virtue of transnational interactions and how global citizenship values are fostered through transnational spaces, mutual learning and reciprocal knowledge sharing. While much of the literature on IDVs focuses on capacity building (Machin 2008), the role of IDVs in bringing new forms of expertise, and the cosmopolitan values experienced by IDVs, the findings from this research emphasize the agency of partner organizations in creating reciprocity and mutual learning. This paper examines transnationalism, reciprocity, and mutual learning from the perspective of partner organizations and the shift in the dynamics that govern transnational spaces where IDVs and partner organizations interact. As the findings in this study reveal, when it comes to gender equality programming, partner organizations play a central role in demonstrating cosmopolitanism and in advancing transnational feminist priorities. Moreover, this paper shows that the flow of knowledge and information sharing is multi-directional and not unidirectional (not limited to North-to-South knowledge sharing), and therefore the lens of cosmopolitanism in transnational spaces is important for understanding how change happens.

2. Literature Review

International development volunteering is recognized for the benefits accrued to the international volunteers who are able to enhance their learning, to contribute to greater global awareness, and to promote global citizenship (Chapman 2018). Part of the growing desire to engage in international development volunteering derives from the belief that cross-cultural experiences promote cosmopolitan values and engaged global citizens. However, global citizenship identity is not exclusive to the experiences of sojourners. As I argue in this paper, cosmopolitan identities are shaped by IDV interventions and experienced by both volunteers and partners. This section will define key concepts such as global citizenship and cosmopolitanism, before outlining the literature around the role of IDVs in fostering cosmopolitan identities and highlight the gaps in the literature that this paper will fill.

2.1 Global Citizenship and Cosmopolitanism

The literature on international development volunteering is replete with references to global citizenship, yet the term is rarely defined or explained by those using it. In fact, the term is frequently used in university settings, among civil society organizations, in development discourse, and in the public sector to characterize our moral obligations to the rest of humanity, a common identity, and way of living that recognizes and promotes international solidarity (Tiessen/Huish 2014; Cameron 2014). Unfortunately, as various scholars have noted, the term is often contested, elusive, vague, and associated with many contradictory definitions with almost no grounding in the political, philosophical, and ethical debates that might give the concept real meaning (Cameron 2014; Shultz 2007; Tiessen/Epprecht 2012). The range of possible meanings for global citizenship suggests that the term relies heavily on its conceptual vagueness (Lewin, 2009). In some definitions, individuals link their identity of global citizenship to notions of personal growth combined with other measures of societal change, while in others, global citizenship is defined as the ability to travel and live in other cultural contexts and to enhance intercultural relations (Heron/Tiessen 2012). It is important to note that how global citizenship is defined shapes the kind of experiences that volunteers have and encounter. For example, if global citizenship is framed and theorized as a method of 'helping' and 'saving' partners in the Global South, programming will inadvertently generate a narrative of global citizenship that reinforces neocolonial attitudes and neoliberal globalization (Rennick 2013).

For the purposes of this paper, I draw on the definition of 'global citizenship' from Heron and Tiessen (2007), who describe this as a way of understanding the world in which an individual's *attitudes and behaviours* reflect empathy for those marginalized and a concern for the relationship between poverty and wealth – within and between communities, countries, and regions..

The term global citizenship is part of a broader conception of global cosmopolitanism which denotes a new regionalism, or a strengthened global civil society supported by a new "normative architecture" of world order values (Tiessen/Epprecht 2012). Cosmopolitanism emphasizes the role of community on the global level as well as the formation of global norms. At the heart of cosmopolitanism is the conviction that by virtue of simply being human, all humans have certain moral obligations toward all other human beings (Cameron 2014). As an ideal, cosmopolitanism expresses the idea that all human beings – regardless of national, religious, cultural, or political affiliation – should be seen as members of the same community, and that this community should be cultivated. Likewise, cosmopolitan values put emphasis not just on positive moral obligations, but also on negative obligations to not cause harm, not benefit from harm, and to work to prevent harm (Cameron 2014). In other words, cosmopolitanism focuses on restructuring systems to reduce harm by putting heavy emphasis on the personal responsibility of all humans to be aware of the consequences of their actions on other humans.

It is important to note that many scholars (Cameron 2014; Dobson 2006; Linklater 2007) differentiate between 'thick' and 'thin' understandings of cosmopolitanism. Dobson (2006) argues that "thin conceptions of cosmopolitanism revolve around compassion for the vulnerable but leave asymmetries of power and wealth intact [whereas] thick conceptions of cosmopolitanism attempt to influence the structural conditions faced by vulnerable groups" (2006: 169). In essence, thick conceptions of cosmopolitanism call for informed and sustained political action aimed at ending the suffering of others in which we are implicated. On the other hand, thin conceptions of cosmopolitanism (e.g., international travel, volunteer work, and building skills) focus on the specific skills international volunteers (IVs) foster without situating those values and skills in the broader theoretical, ethical, and political context in which global justice is achieved. The next section will outline the role of International Development Volunteer (IDV) programs in promoting global citizenship and cosmopolitanism values.

2.2 IDVs, Thick Global Citizenship, and Cosmopolitanism Values

The scope for IDV programs to enhance global citizenship and cosmopolitan values in participants builds on the expectation that cross-cultural experiences with distant 'others' will lead to a greater openness to difference – a more cosmopolitan disposition (Vertovec/Cohen 2002). The narrative supporting this understanding is that IDVs are more likely to adopt a cosmopolitan outlook because they are more overtly exposed to cultures, values and places that they experience as foreign vis-à-vis their own cultural frames of reference (Rovisco 2009). This narrative, which focuses on the importance of building cosmopolitan identities through international volunteering, informs the rise of IDVs engaged in transnational interactions. However, many scholars question the expected impact of enhanced cosmopolitanism, noting that thin conceptions of global citizenship that may result often fail to grapple with the theoretical origins of the term. To motivate IDVs towards 'thicker' connections of cosmopolitan action, Linklater (2007) argues that volunteers must believe that they are causally responsible for harming others and their physical environment. Building off this argument, Dobson (2006) argues that "we are more likely to feel obliged to assist others in their plight if we are responsible for their situation – if there is some identifiable causal relationship between what we do, or what we have done, and how they are" (2006: 171). In other words, Dobson and Linklater both argue that it is in fact causal responsibility that fosters "thicker connections" between people and helps to shift beyond "the territory of beneficence and into the realm of justice" (Dobson 2006: 172). Moreover, thick conceptions of cosmopolitanism highlight the ways in which privileged citizens and consumers in the Global North are implicated in the global production of poverty and oppression (e.g., through unfair global trade rules and access to cheap material goods at the expense of communities in the Global South). This linkage and conceptualization of thick cosmopolitanism reinforces the debates around moral responsibilities and obligations.

The debate around IDVs developing cosmopolitan identities and values often focuses on the values experienced by the volunteers and rarely focuses on how intercultural experiences shape new cosmopolitan identities with the partner organizations receiving volunteers. This paper will focus on the latter by analyzing the changing cosmopolitanism identities of partner organizations in the Global South that engage with IDVs. I argue that IDVs play a pivotal role in transnational spaces and that cross-cultural encounters, reciprocal learning, and experiences of transnationalism need also to be examined from the perspective of those who 'receive' volunteers. These transnational encounters have specific implications for changing attitudes and cosmopolitan perspectives around gender equality and feminism and contribute to our understanding of trans-cultural relations for which culture is viewed as dynamic and fluid, and individuals carry different cultures that are not bound only to a nation-state or a region.

Gender equality has been a global priority for more than 40 years, since the adoption and ratification of the United Nations Convention on the Elimination of all forms of Discrimination against Women (CEDAW) in 1981. The 1995 Beijing conference and the resulting Beijing Platform for Action further laid out the priorities for a more equitable world that recognizes women's rights as human rights. Cosmopolitan priorities to advance gender equality can also be found in the Sustainable Development Goals (SDGs), specifically Goal 5 to Achieve Gender Equality and Empower all Women and Girls. These global priorities reflect the significance of a cosmopolitan vision for gender equality in the coming together of people from different countries to promote justice and equality for all. As a result of these global commitments, there has been an increase in IDVs working on gender-related projects, building capacity of gender-related themes, and working closely with local feminist organizations.

3. Methods

Interviews were conducted in 2018 – 2019 with 150 partner organization staff in ten countries. Once all interviews were transcribed, data were coded to identify common themes throughout. The introduction to this special edition has more detailed information on the methodology for data collection and the analysis of findings.

4. Findings

Drawing on the interviews, this paper shines light on the changing cosmopolitan perspectives and global citizenship views of partner organizations that are developed as a result of with the transnational interactions with IDVs. Specifically, the research found that IDVs play a role in transnational spaces that further develop cosmopolitan values and that global citizenship values and understandings are enhanced through these transnational spaces through mutual learning and reciprocal knowledge sharing. The findings highlight five main themes: shifts in attitudes and behaviours towards gender equality; new insights and fresh ideas arising from interactions with IDVs; skills-building; the development of long-term relationships of reciprocity and mutual learning; and tensions between partner organizations and transnational interactions. Tensions are examined as they relate to the need for ongoing negotiation and mutual learning in these collaborative, transnational interactions.

One of the main findings that came out of this research was the role that cross-cultural exchange plays in building the capacity to shift attitudes and behaviours towards enhanced gender equality. Participants in this study often mentioned that dialogue with IDVs during workshops, casual conversations, and meeting reflections has given them the space to consider gender equality differently and to identify opportunities where gender equality can be mainstreamed into practice. The cross-cultural exchange was seen to have particular value in relation to advancing new insights and bringing in fresh ideas. One of the respondents in Tanzania mentioned the value of new ideas as a result of people coming from various environments and providing a new perception on gender equality, noting: "We need very fresh eyes on some old stuff so that we can modify or do them better. They say, if you are doing something for a very long time, you might develop monotony. Fresh eyes help us develop."

The Tanzanian participant went on to explain that these fresh insights are combined with locally-based understanding: "These experiences we are sharing from their country and our country, our perception of things, it develops both of us". The shared learning arises from each party having an opportunity to share their knowledge with each other: "[T]hey say what they have and [we say] what we have, we look at the gap and advocate to [fill it]. Through these interactions partner organization staff come to understand what is possible and what they can advocate for: "The results, we understand that we need to advocate more or to do more work so that we can achieve a sustainable gender equality, or gender equity which is present in their countries. Or we can have some sort of similarities but with regard to our culture also."

The contribution of fresh perspectives and ideas between IDVs and partner organizations around gender equality contributes to the breaking down of stereotypes or preconceived gender norms and towards enhancing cosmopolitan values among partner organizations. The diverse perspectives that IDVs contribute support partner organizations in identifying ways their practices and programs can mainstream gender equality. For example, in Ghana, one staff member of a partner organization noted the importance of IDVs who "insist we make sure they are gender sensitive such that it won't be all male or all female [in trainings]". This influence results in greater attention to all members of staff, their diverse roles and responsibilities and the need for better inclusion and equitable participation. While the focus here is on a gender-sensitive approach to programming focused on access and participation in training, our research found that IDVs were working towards building more nuanced understandings of gender equality, one that moved passed a liberal understanding.

Similarly, in Ghana the participating organization mentioned that IDVs bring new insights that encourage them to think about their practices differently. Building on the themes above, partner organizations refer to the influential role of IDVs who challenge partner organizations to ensure greater gender equality among their program beneficiaries. As the study participant from Ghana noted: "Gender equality has in a way improved since we started receiving the international volunteers in this organisation. They started pushing us that 'why do we have only men holding higher position and women are not if they have the qualification?'" The partner organizations used these opportunities to consider their program approach and to challenge themselves to advance gender equality in their programs by focussing on both male and female small-holder farmers. The participant concluded that the IDVs played a substantial role in helping the partner organization understand their work through a gender lens.

The capacity built through these relationships demonstrates the importance of relationship building and shared experiences through cross-cultural exchange. Specifically, the ways in which new perspectives and dialogue can help shift attitudes and breakdown stereotypes. Within the structural limitations of unequal systems and power structures, diverse experiences including opportunities, entry points, and development outcomes can be addressed in dialogue.

One of the many roles IDVs play during their placement is to build capacity in their host organization across a spectrum of specializations and competencies. These skills include interpersonal skills; communication and technical writing; leadership training; gender equality training; computer literacy; and language training, among other skills. In this collection, Sadat provides a summary of the breadth of skills transferred and capacities built through IDV interactions. These skills and interactions with IDVs have supported partner organizations to reflect on their role in transnational spaces, their role in supporting gender equality, and also their role in enhancing global citizenship values. For example, in Peru, the participant organization mentioned that their interactions with IDVs encouraged them to reflect and discuss themes around controversial topics while also identifying ways to develop the capacity to learn how to communicate and address these difficult conversations with the community. The example of sensitive topics such as abortion was raised as one way that IDVs have created spaces to speak more openly about important topics. As the individual from Peru notes: "Here there was fear to speak on the theme of abortion, but we have conversed on how to approach this. We have reflected and developed capacities within ourselves." The IDV, in this example, played an important role in helping the partner organization to translate their own feminist values and approaches into an understanding and conversation about abortion.

The findings highlight that the cross-cultural exchange with IDVs help partner organizations develop skills (both soft and hard skills) to integrate gender equality. Their exposure to the perspectives of IDVs has given partner organizations the opportunity to enhance their own skills and capacities and identify opportunities to integrate their learning to the local community. For example, an organization from Kenya stated that as a result of IDVs, the organization was able to develop gender sensitive policies around employment. Similarly, they were able to identify ways that they could use the internet to support the local women's market and increase their selling capacity. Of significance, however, is the way that skills – and capacity – building is viewed by the partner organizations in a cosmopolitan manner, not as an imposition from outside. The participants highlighted how the reciprocity of learning from each other's experiences created a transnational flow of gender equality because IDVs learned from the experiences of the partner organizations and vice versa. Further, in Kenya, one study participant (a member of a partner organization) spoke about the ways that cultural information is shared between partners and IDVs. They note that "people learn about our culture, and we learn about their culture, so there's no misconceptions or stereotypes." This interviewee noticed a change in their perspective from "interacting with [people from other communities around the world] and having time with them" it's totally changed my perspective." Moreover, the study participant goes on to suggest that every organization should benefit from these transnational encounters and sharing of knowledge, suggesting that many more people should "travel abroad and volunteer and get to learn about many different communities." Therefore, the learning and capacity building resulting from interactions with IDVs was not seen as one-directional. Rather, the findings from this research highlight the reciprocity and mutual learning of cosmopolitan values that happen in these transnational spaces.

The idea of mutual learning and knowledge sharing is understood as one that continues even after the IDV returns home. As one participant from Malawi noted, IDVs can continue to share their skills and what they have learned after they return home. The knowledge sharing also includes ways that Malawians have been able to "equip" IDVs with knowledge about Malawian cultural practices. The participant reinforced the significance of "exchange of experiences and innovative ideas." Beyond an emphasis on mutual learning is the significance accorded to the transnational flow of ideas that is multi-directional. The partner organization staff, as one study participant from Kenya notes, are "also giving them some skills also teaching them, you know it is kind of a two-way thing, they also learn."

The reciprocity and mutual learning that is created as a result of intercultural relations and interactions with IVDs has led to new cosmopolitan identities among partner organizations. Many partner organizations feel that the relationships they have built with IDVs have enhanced their cosmopolitanism and their views around gender equality. The key message shared by the participants in this research is that as an organization they are always in a learning environment, therefore anyone who enters that environment brings with them their skills and expertise but also leaves with skills and expertise from the organization. This reciprocity and mutual learning help formulate new identities both amongst the volunteers and amongst the partner organizations.

While this research has found that the cross-cultural exchange between IDVs and partner organizations supports the building of cosmopolitan identities among both stakeholders, the findings also demonstrate that there are limitations. IDVs can also reinforce cultural tensions in their efforts to promote gender equality where activities challenge gender norms or are perceived to challenge "tradition and culture". In Malawi, some partner organizations believed that IDVs were wasting their time trying to change the gender norms of the community because the communities would continue to see IDVs as "outsiders" and would not pay attention to calls for changing societal norms.

The emphasis being made by the partner organization in Malawi was that it is best for IDVs to focus their energy on training a number of community members and those community members working with the broader community on gender equality because they are insiders and know how to navigate the power dynamics that are embedded in community structures. Likewise, partner organization staff in several countries, including Ghana, Tanzania, and Malawi emphasized the importance of IDVs understanding the local context in which they are working to advance gender equality in order to ensure their work is sustained. As one organization in Malawi stated:

> *[...] when getting engaged in any country, first of all [you] should have a lot of knowledge about the culture of that particular country. If volunteers come without that knowledge, it will compromise our culture. They should know a lot [about] the country where they are going and understand the gap that is there on gender so that when they come, they are not there for a gender intervention [but], should be there as part of society to learn more, if then intervention should come on top of what you have already learnt [that's great]. Otherwise coming for the intervention, we want to change this and that, I don't think it can work.*

This finding emphasizes that the perception of a lack of understanding IDVs have on the local culture and the resistance some community members may have toward initiatives try to advance gender equality. Further concerns were identified by partner organization staff in Ghana who highlighted the challenges arising from IDVs engaged in gender equality work when the programs leave men out. Shahadu Bitamsimli (this volume) addresses this in greater detail, noting that not all partner organization staff embrace outsider interventions on gender equality and women's empowerment, particularly when local men are not actively involved in finding solutions to gender problems. This finding reinforces the importance of understanding local culture, structures of power, key actors, and key spaces to navigate and advance gender equality. This was highlighted in a conversation with a partner organization in Peru that stated:

> *Firstly, and fundamentally, it is important to understand as much as possible and as quickly as possible, the history of Peru and to not make conclusions. As I said, it is one of the most violent countries against women, there is no justification for this, but there are ways to understand. And to transform things, you need to understand and not judge. In the history of 17 years working in social mobilization, with foreigners coming to Peru, they come down from the plane and try to explain why you live how you live... [IVs should] give more time to try to understand why we live in this chaos before giving answers.*

This finding outline one of the key struggles and cultural tensions that exist between IDVs and partner organizations who work to address gender equality. Strategies to support gender equality cannot simply be imported and transmitted transnationally. This was reinforced by a partner organization in Ghana who stated that the IDVs' understanding of gender equality "is not possible to implement here [in Ghana] because we have our own culture and our own way of gender equality which is to create equal opportunities for women". These findings demonstrate the importance of transnational knowledge-sharing in ways that are respectful of local knowledge and cultural practices. While there was clear evidence among some of the study participants to the role of IDVs in the promotion of gender equality, the majority of the study participants highlighted opportunities for mutual learning and knowledge sharing so that the insights and ideas that IDVs bring could be incorporated into local knowledge and cultural realities.

Gender equality programming must be adapted and applied to the local context in ways that are informed and understood by the local community. This point reinforces the importance of mutual learning and reciprocity between IDVs and partner organizations as methods to reduce cultural tensions and increase new cosmopolitan identities.

5. Analysis

The findings highlight a shift in the dynamics that govern transnational spaces where IDVs and partner organizations interact. While much of the literature on IDVs focus on capacity building and the role of IDVs in bringing new forms of knowledge and expertise, the findings from this research emphasize the agency of partner organizations in creating reciprocity and mutual learning. In other words, the nature of the relationship between IDVs and partner organization is no longer framed or experienced as a unidirectional flow of ideas and experiences (Lough et al. 2009; Machin 2008). Rather, this research found that partner organizations view themselves as having the resources and the capacity to also give back to the volunteers. In fact, when it came to gender equality programming, partner organizations emphasized that IDVs required the knowledge of the organization to better understand the context and the approach to addressing gender equality. In other words, the shift in dynamic focused on IDVs working with partner organizations to enhance gender equality rather than replacing the work of partner organizations. This approach positioned partner organizations as active recipients engaging in a truly reciprocal exchange model, where neither actor is given exclusive benefit; give and take is expected from both sides (Hartman et al. 2014; Palacios 2010). In other words, the findings show that partner organizations in the Global South believe that mutual exchange and reciprocity actively exists among themselves and IDVs. This reciprocity as a mutual benefit was key in this research as it helped reduce the power differences that often exist in these transnational spaces. As Lough and Oppenheim (2017) argue, when reciprocity is low, volunteering as 'service' tends to reinforce power differences between giver and receiver – often in equal measure to other conventional aid relationships. However, in this research, the participant organizations acknowledged and argued for the importance of their role in these spaces and in their ability to effectively enhance gender equality both within their organization and in the communities where they work.

The emphasis on mutual learning and reciprocity is supported by the assumption that "poor" people are best positioned to know how to articulate their problems, priorities, and the results of international projects (Narayan et al. 2000). This was clear in the numerous times participants in this research mentioned the need for local community members to discuss issues of gender equality rather than trainings run by IDVs, because as insiders the local community members know the tensions, problems, and priorities best. This finding further emphasizes the significance of the agency and voice of partner organizations. Specifically, highlighting the role partner organizations have played in transforming the spaces of intercultural exchange from one of imbalanced power – where IDVs would prescribe development outcomes and interpret the reality of local communities based on their own knowledge – towards one that reflects a more balanced exchange of knowledge, where Southern partner organizations are in the position to demand their voices be heard and to accurately interpret their own complex reality. As partner organizations have gained more experience working with IDVs and have built relationships with Northern partners, there is a shift in these transnational spaces where alternative voices are equally valued and legitimized, and where more authentic relations of reciprocity are able to form. Having the agency to choose how partner organizations like to advance gender equality, and how they best see the role of IDVs in their community, demonstrates that partner organizations are now in a position to carve out an understanding of how they wish to be represented rather than having their perspectives imposed upon them (Tiessen/Lough/Cheung 2018).

The shift in transnational space and the role of IDVs and partner organizations has been possible because of the rise of cosmopolitanism, a transnational mode of practice whereby actors construct bonds of mutual commitment and reciprocity across borders through public discourse and socio-political struggle (Cameron 2014). The relationships that partner organizations are making with IDVs in promoting a transnational flow of ideas on gender equality is in fact creating a 'cosmopolitanism from below'. This cosmopolitanism from below is premised on the multiplicity of experiences, the simultaneous existence of multilayered local, national, and global identities rather than to the notion of egalitarian universalism (Kurasawa 2004). As such, IDVs play a role in these transnational spaces to develop cosmopolitan values through relationship building, intercultural interactions, and listening to the voices of partner organizations. In this way, IDVs can support cosmopolitanism from below by learning and listening to the experiences of partner organizations in their efforts to advance gender equality, and forging links and networks with civic associations in both the Global North and the Global South to support these efforts. While the literature has focused on cosmopolitan values experienced by IDVs that privilege notions of global citizenship that seek to advance ideas of global solidarity through universalist conceptions, this research found that transnational interactions between IDVs and partner organizations are creating a new cosmopolitan from below that is characterized by identities that privilege bonds of mutuality and reciprocity between partners in different parts of the globe. This cosmopolitanism from below is advanced through the understanding that global solidarity can be derived from transnational webs of affinity that are themselves formed out of individuals and groups participating in processes of discussion and argumentation aiming to negotiate a common political terrain (Kurasawa 2004). As we saw in this research, partner organizations were seeking to advance gender equality on their own terms. While they required and appreciated the support of IDVs in identifying entry points and methods to approach gender equality, in the end, participants in this study found that it was insiders of the community that needed to do the negotiating, mobilizing, and advocacy to see change. This broader understanding of cosmopolitanism, a cosmopolitanism from below, informed by reciprocal learning, intercultural interactions, and transnationalism, is what is required in order to sustainably advance gender equality.

6. Conclusion

The findings analyzed in this paper consider the experiences of partner organizations in transnational spaces and the nature of reciprocity and mutual exchange in supporting gender equality programming. The research found that when it comes to gender equality programming, partner organizations have demonstrated their agency to advance feminist priorities while also advocating for the necessary components to achieve gender equality, and to be at the forefront of this change. This research found that partner organizations view themselves as having the resources and the capacity to advance gender equality programming – particularly when supported by IDVs – and that these transnational spaces should no longer be framed as spaces where there is a unidirectional flow of ideas and experiences.

Instead, this research found that transnational actors play a role in creating cosmopolitan identities in transnational spaces of mutual learning and reciprocity. In fact, transnational actors influence and benefit from transnational spaces to enhance their cosmopolitan views (impacts that are felt by IDVs and partner organizations alike). These transactions of knowledge and mutual learning are important for advancing gender equality and women's empowerment because it helps improve understandings of agency and structural realities. Specifically, it has helped partner communities both work within their own cultural communities as well as in transnational spaces with IDVs to facilitate changes towards social justice and support a 'cosmopolitanism from below'. This understanding provides nuance to understanding the relationship of IDVs with partner organizations as one that is multilayered with a multiplicity of experiences working towards an egalitarian universalism. In the efforts to advance gender equality, framing the relationship of IDVs and partner organizations as one that supports a 'cosmopolitanism from below' allows for an experience based on learning, listening, and empowering.

Bibliography

Cameron, John (2014): Grounding experiential learning in "thick" conceptions of global citizenship. In: Tiessen, Rebecca; Huish, Robert (ed.): Globetrotting or Global Citizenship? Perils and Potential of International Experiential Learning. Toronto, pp. 21-42.

Chapman, Deborah (2018): The ethics of international service learning as a pedagogical development practice: A Canadian study. In: Third World Quarterly, vol. 39, no. 10, pp. 1899-1922.

Dobson, Andrew (2006): Thick cosmopolitanism. In: Political Studies, vol. 54, pp. 165–184.

Hartman, Eric; Paris, Cody Morris; Blache-Cohen, Brandon (2014): Fair Trade Learning: Ethical standards for community-engaged international volunteer tourism. In: Tourism and Hospitality Research, vol. 14, no. 1-2, pp. 108-116.

Heron, Barbara; Tiessen, Rebecca (2007): Creating Global Citizens? The Impact of Learning/ Volunteer Abroad Programs. https://idl-bnc-idrc.dspacedirect.org/handle/10625/51024?-show=full (3.10.2021).

Kurasawa, Fuyuki (2004): A Cosmopolitanism from below: Alternative globalization and the creation of a solidarity without bounds. In: European Journal of Sociology, vol. 45, no. 2, pp. 233-255.

Lewin, Ross (2009): The handbook of practice and research in study abroad: Higher education and the quest for global citizenship. New York.

Linklater, Andrew (2007): Distant suffering and cosmopolitan obligations. In: International Politics, vol. 44, no. 1, pp. 19-36.

Lough, Benjamin J.; McBridge, Amanda Moore; Sherraden, Margaret S. (2009): Perceived effects of international volunteering. https://www.brookings.edu/wp-content/uploads/2016/06/0621_volunteering_mcbride.pdf (2.10.2021)

Lough, Benjamin. J.; Oppenheim, Willy (2017): Revisiting reciprocity in international volunteering. In: Progress in Development Studies, vol. 17, no. 3, pp. 197-213.

Machin, Joanna (2008): The impact of returned international volunteers on the UK: A scoping review. http://build-online.org.uk/documents/Impact%20of%20International%20Volunteering%20on%20the%20UK%20VSO%20Machin%202008-1.pdf (3.10.2021).

Narayan, Deepa; Patel, Raj; Schafft, Kai; Rademacher, Anne; Koch-Schulte, Sarah (2000): Voices of the poor: Can anyone hear us? New York.

Palacios, Carlos (2010): Volunteer tourism, development and education in a postcolonial world: Conceiving global connections beyond aid. In: Journal of Sustainable Tourism, vol. 18, pp. 861-878.

Rennick, Joanne (2013): Towards a pedagogy of good global citizenship. In: Rennick, Joanne Benham; Desjardins, Michel (ed.): The world is my classroom: International learning and Canadian higher education. Toronto, pp. 3-15.

Rovisco, Maria (2009): Religion and the challenges of cosmopolitanism: Young Portuguese volunteers in Africa. In: Nowicka, Magdalena; Rovisco, Maria (ed.): Cosmopolitanism in practice. Farnham, pp. 181-199.

Shultz, Lynette (2007): Educating for global citizenship: Conflicting agendas and understandings. In: Alberta Journal of Educational Research, vol. 53, no. 3, pp. 248–258.

Tiessen, Rebecca; Epprecht, Marc (2012): Introduction: Global citizenship education for learning/volunteering abroad. In: Journal of Global Citizenship & Equity Education, vol. 2, no. 1, pp. 1-10.

Tiessen, Rebecca; Lough, Bejamin J.; Cheung, Samuel (2018): Introduction: A theoretical and methodological case for examining agency and power relations in North-South volunteering research collaborations. In: Tiessen, Rebecca; Lough, Benjamin J.; Grantham, Kate (ed.): Insights on International Volunteering. Perspectives From the Global South. Germany, pp. 7-12.

Vertovec, Steven; Cohen, Robin (2002): Conceiving cosmopolitanism: theory, context and practice. Oxford.

Organizational Commitments to Gender Equality Programming: Resistance, Externalizing, and Opportunities for Gender Mainstreaming

Lan Thi Nguyen

1. Introduction

Gender inequality is one of the most significant human rights challenges of our time (UN Women: n.d.). Women are disproportionately affected by higher poverty rates, gender-based violence, child marriage, and early mortality with adolescent births. Building on previous international commitments designed to put women's rights and gender equality as a cross-cutting theme in international development, the Beijing Platform for Action (arising out of the 1995 Beijing Conference) prioritized several areas of action needed to promote women's rights and gender equality. Among these priorities, the Platform highlighted the issue of gender mainstreaming strategies and gender equality programming. These priorities have increasingly been adopted by non-governmental organizations (NGOs) and civil society organizations (CSOs) since the 1995 Beijing Conference.

Before the conference, other international commitments also called for more significant investments in women's rights, such as the Convention on the Elimination of Discrimination against Women (CEDAW) – an international treaty adopted in 1979 by the United Nations General Assembly ratified by 189 countries. More recent commitments to gender equality can be found in the 2000 Millennium Development Goals (MDGs, particularly Goal 3: To Promote Gender Equality and Empower Women) and the updated international priorities under the Sustainable Development Goals (SDGs, particularly Goal 5: Gender Equality) which was adopted by 193 countries. All ten countries examined in this study (Malawi, Kenya, Nepal, Uganda, Senegal, Ghana, Vietnam, Peru, Guatemala, and Tanzania) have agreed to and ratified these international commitments while also committing to designing national-level policies, machinery, and services to promote women's empowerment and gender equality. As a signpost of the global solidarity needed to achieve SDG 5, one participant from Uganda noted: "almost all countries have international standards regarding gender equality... We are all striving for the same goal". Development NGOs have demonstrated mixed progress on implementing international priorities to address gender inequality and implement gender mainstreaming strategies (Tiessen 2007).

This paper examines this 'mixed progress' and begins by defining gender mainstreaming and summarizing the contribution of gender mainstreaming to development. Next, an overview of the relevant literature highlights the problems and possibilities for improved (or transformative) gender mainstreaming, and then considers how development NGOs in the Global South have navigated gender equality priorities concerning resistance, externalizing, and integration of gender mainstreaming with support from international development volunteers (IDVs). The paper then turns to explore the diverse experiences of development NGOs concerning gender mainstreaming priorities, with attention to resistance elements to adopting gender equality and women's empowerment (GEWE) programming. Findings are buttressed by examples of opportunities for advancing GEWE through innovative programming within the partner organizations that support and guide IDVs. Finally, the paper analyzes activities that externalize (project gender inequality issues onto rural communities, rather than internalizing gender equality priorities within the development organizations) GEWE priorities to activities in rural or remote communities and conclude with implications for practice.

2. Literature Review

GEWE has a long history dating back to international commitments and conventions. The record includes the 1979 Convention on the Elimination of all Forms of Discrimination against Women (CEDAW), the Beijing Platform for Action (1995), and more recently, the MDGs and SDGs. The Beijing Platform for Action, in particular, outlined the need for a gender mainstreaming approach to ensure that "gender perspectives and attention to the goal of gender equality are central to all activities – policy development, research, advocacy/dialogue, legislation, resource allocation, and planning, implementation and monitoring of programmes and projects" (UN Women: n.d.).

The Beijing Platform for Action prioritized gender mainstreaming as the mechanism to achieve gender equality. Two critical aspects of different definitions of gender mainstreaming exist: (1) the institutionalization of gender concerns and experiences within the organization and (2) women's empowerment (Moser/Moser 2005). To fully integrate gender priorities requires considering GEWE in administrative, financial, human resources management, and other organizational procedures, leading to a long-term transformation in staff's attitudes, behaviors, cultures, and operations (Tiessen 2007). Gender empowerment means promoting women's participation in decision-making processes, making their voices heard, recognizing that women have agency, ability, and capacity to make choices and make decisions related to their own lives (Moser/Moser 2005).

Despite clear definitions and national commitments to gender mainstreaming, development organizations have been slow to adopt gender-sensitive programs and priorities. Some of the reasons attributed to the slow uptake of gender mainstreaming are lack of staff capacity and training in gender equality, an organizational culture that prevents GEWE, and negative attitudes among staff toward women or gender priorities (Derbyshire 2002; Moser/Moser 2005). However, effective gender mainstreaming practice within development organizations requires a broad range of commitments, from human resource policies such as anti-discrimination policies, budget allocations to integrate gender equality across diverse program priorities, staff training opportunities, coordinated efforts across the organization with support from gender-trained experts, and operational practices that mainstream gender equality into programs, projects, and activities (Jahan 1995). Examples of operational gender mainstreaming practices include increasing focus on the gender-related impacts in project design implementation and evaluation of projects and programs, sex-disaggregated data collection, and gender analysis to ensure that projects/programs can challenge unequal power relations.

The success of gender mainstreaming activities relies heavily on all members' internal responsibility and commitments within organizations, including all staff. It also demands careful attention to masculinist or patriarchal organizational cultures that perpetuate negative attitudes, working environments, and practices that discriminate against women staff and community beneficiaries (Valk 2000; Rao/Kelleher 2016). Examples of exclusionary practices include organizational practices that may not reflect the needs of those who are responsible for childcare (Wallace 1998). There are also examples of forms of resistance and "backlash" to gender equality and gender mainstreaming, such as denial of the issue of gender inequality and lack of awareness of gender issues (Flood et al. 2020).

Even when efforts are in place for mainstreaming gender within development organizations, bureaucratic norms and practices may prevent gender equality priorities from translating from policy goals to bureaucratic performance and program delivery (Tiessen 2019). Moreover, bureaucratic norms and practices may result in neoliberal and instrumentalist techniques of governance (Eerdewijk/Davids 2014), resulting in checking boxes of gender indicators to meet a requirement rather than meaningful change to policy and practice. Thus, achieving a 'transformative' vision of gender mainstreaming requires institutional change and addressing the masculinist status quo within institutions and development organizations (Parpart 2014). This framing explores how partner organizations navigate gender mainstreaming with support from international development volunteers in the Global South.

3. Methods

Interviews were conducted in 2018 – 2019 with 150 partner organization staff in ten countries. Once all interviews were transcribed, data were coded to identify common themes throughout data analysis. Finally, data were analyzed using discourse analysis. The introduction to this special edition has more detailed information on the methodology for data collection and the study of findings.

4. Findings

Three significant findings frame the analysis of the diverse experiences of these staff members, including (1) challenges and resistance to gender mainstreaming; (2) externalizing priorities for transformative change in gender relations as a problem occurring "somewhere else" in rural and remote areas, and (3) opportunities for improved gender awareness in transnational spaces.

4.1 Challenges and Resistance to Gender Mainstreaming in Partner Organizations

Some of the partner organization staff acknowledged that gender is not the main focus of their work. Therefore, they do not have many activities related to promoting gender equality and gender mainstreaming. Feedback received from a Vietnam-based partner organization staff demonstrated rationales provided by some development organizations for why gender was not perceived as an essential lens for their work. For example, for one organization with a "focus on hospitality management, restaurant management," gender equality is not considered an important area of focus since their activities are seen as gender-neutral. Likewise, another participant from Vietnam noted: "There is no difference between men and women, male and female, there is no program focusing on gender, as we respect 'diversity' suggesting that all students are treated fairly and equally, even in organizations where fewer than 10 percent of their participants involved in information technology training are women. The main area of focus was to increase overall enrollments with little consideration for the lack of interest in their programs from diverse groups.

Other participants considered gender equality programming as not their priority in terms of organizational work. As a participant from Guatemala noted, "the culture of the superiority of men is talked about sometimes. But we don't talk about these things in the organization [or] in our offices. This is not part of what we do". The participant explained that respect for women and commitments to gender equality were highly valued within the organization, but these commitments were not linked to organization commitments, policies, or actions.

Several participants from different countries referred to perceive success at the national level in achieving gender equality. For example, in Vietnam and Nepal, several participants noted that gender equality had been achieved already in the country, citing education enrollments of boys and girls and legal mechanisms in those countries, as a participant from Nepal noted, "both men and women are equal in our law, and we also treat them equally in our school."

These findings highlight a perception among some partner organization staff that gender mainstreaming is not a priority at the organizational level, and little if any time is devoted to addressing organizational practices that might contribute to program design biases or inequality in the treatment of certain staff members. For organizations that do not see their programs as specific to gender equality projects, gender issues were considered irrelevant and the focus of other organizations. Some of the limited contributions to gender mainstreaming in their organizations were explained as a lack of capacity to do this type of work. Interviewees noted that they faced challenges in carrying out gender mainstreaming due to their limited understanding of gender issues and their lack of expertise and confidence to work on issues of gender equality. One interview participant from Vietnam noted that their organization lacked the capacity and expertise to work on gender issues, so they relied on partner organizations to bring in that expertise. Partnering with UN Women allowed one organization to design better its training programs with gender equality priorities in mind.

Several organizations also mentioned the need for gender training, noting that donor or partner organizations in the Global North often provided some level of training. However, due to limited time, financial, and human resources, gender training and capacity building for staff have been limited. In addition, leadership in partner organizations has not made gender training a priority.

During several interviews, when asked if the organization has strategies to address GEWE, organizational staff referred to data about the percentage of women who had participated in events. In several countries, partner organizations referred to their reporting guidelines and commitment to recording women and men as beneficiaries of training or project activities.

However, these strategies of recording sex-disaggregated data did not often include strategies to understand why the inclusion of women or diverse groups was necessary, nor did they consider the nature of their participation, nor the impacts of the activities in relation to gender issues. In each project report for Canadian funders, partner organizations are required to provide information about how their programs have addressed gender issues. However, when being asked about how they completed such reports, several partner organizations highlighted how they included only the number of women who attended activities.

Addressing the structural inequality and social norms and beliefs that perpetuate gender inequality were generally not discussed due to limited awareness and understanding of broader gender issues and the tendency among partner organizations to focus on individuals rather than societal realities. For example, organization staff talked about the importance of ensuring gender balance in the number of participants. Furthermore, annual reports recorded the number of male and female participants and, in some cases, information about salaries for men and women. A respondent from Vietnam noted: "the number of the female teachers is the same as male teachers, and the rate salary is the same... That is the way we deal with gender."

Interviewees sometimes demonstrated resistance or refusal to consider gender issues in their work. The resistance was often linked to narrow perceptions of what constitutes equality. For example, in Vietnam, a participant noted: "There is no difference in the salaries of men and women, women might get higher when they have higher position and experience, [or demonstrated] effectiveness." In other reflections on gender equality, participants shared a limited understanding of gender inequality by linking success to the strength and hard work of the individuals rather than to supportive environments. For example, as one participant noted, "in Vietnam,... female members are not weak. Female lecturers and students undertake many important and hard responsibilities." These examples did not include consideration of the gender division of labor that can take place within workplaces (additional labor women may need to complete as part of their service roles) or the excessive workload they may experience in their homes (taking on more responsibilities caring for children and other family members). Despite these views of success being linked to hard work, some of these same respondents did observe that women lack voice or decision-making power, particularly in some of the highest positions of the organizations where women are less likely to be represented. While gender inequality was observed within the highest positions within the organization, some participants viewed this as generational and changing. As a participant from Vietnam explained: "Our next generation of our younger sisters/ our daughters will be different." The participant considered these changes emerging as young women in the country had different views about their relationships to their husbands and their demand for greater equality. While this was viewed as the vision for the future, "in reality in Vietnam now ... there is still gender inequality even in [the] office".

Other examples of resistance to improving or increasing organizational commitments to gender equality pointed to observations that women are treated better than men or that women and girls are given preferential treatment. In Ghana, some participants referred to programs that provide assistance to women and girls and thereby leave men behind. Participants expressed resistance to a greater focus on gender equality because they perceived too much attention focussed on women and girls already.

Other examples of perceived preferential treatment for women were noted in relation to the "two celebration days for women: one for Vietnam [Day] and one for

International Women's Day. It means that we care enough for everyone... [and that, in fact, the woman] dominates the family". The reference to these two days of celebration of women was seen as a commitment off respect for women. The perception of equal treatment between men and women also translated into perceptions of the equal treatment of girls and boys in the country. As one participant noted, with family sizes being smaller, "the boys and girls are equally treated." Importantly, both boys and girls were sent to school to get a better education in this community. However, a preference for sons was seen by interviewees as a possibility for families who already have a daughter. Otherwise, both boys and girls were generally believed to be treated equally.

In Uganda, participant organization staff referred to new conflicts arising between men and women in the workplace. The concern was that gender equality work, and changes were creating what were perceived to be new inequalities: "I'm seeing a generation where women are more empowered than men, and then we would need to go back to fighting for the rights of men." Another participant from Uganda expressed similar concerns about the "negative consequences" of gender equality work whereby "people feel that maybe women are being promoted, and not the male counterparts." A participant from Kenya expressed concerns that gender equality programming was shifting the balance in favor of women noting that a lot of work is being done for a girl child and "now boys are becoming vulnerable." This change was considered a cause for concern as it could lead to other forms of inequality and bring Kenyan communities "back to where we came from." This growing imbalance was noted by yet an additional participant in Uganda who said: "I'm seeing a generation where women are more empowered than men, and then we need to go back to fighting for the rights of men." The participant concluded that they should focus on equality rather than women's empowerment and avoid being "extremist."

Many of the examples of resistance to discussions of gender equality were explained in reference to cultural practices that highlight men's and women's different roles in society. The most common forms of resistance to gender equality were noted on how the 'beneficiary' communities felt about gender equality and the low level of acceptance of concepts like gender equality in their culture. For example, in Kenya, one participant remarked how society is still: "... steeped in African traditions and is a patriarchal society where men are very dominant and ... women are trying to come to the same level through equality," which can lead to "resistance in this community" by both men and women. According to another participant in Peru, resistance to gender equality was perceived to be a challenge in the projects they implement in the communities where you encounter "machista men" as well as women community members who do not want to disrupt patriarchal norms and who may "close the door" on gender equality programs because the communities do not feel comfortable addressing societal changes to gender relations. In recognition of these multiple areas of resistance within communities, notions of social inclusion and gaining community buy-in were considered essential strategies for addressing gender equality. In the absence of such buy-in, participants referred to the need to tread carefully when doing gender equality work because cultural norms and practices make changes to gender relations a challenge, and gender inequality was generally considered an issue outside the organizations or externalized as elaborated in the section below.

4.2 Perceptions of Gender Inequality as a Problem "Somewhere Else" in Rural and Remote Areas

Perceptions of gender inequality were often directed to problems specific to "other" remote or rural areas. During interviews, many participants began by denying any gender inequality in their cities or their organizations but, throughout the discussion, turned to their perceptions of specific gender-related issues experienced by women as a result of gender inequality in the communities where programs are implemented. For example, one participant from Vietnam referred to support provided to a woman who had become a widow and therefore lost her family income and support, forcing her to commute to the city each day to sell food for survival. When probed, the interviewee began to reflect on why the widow had these discriminatory experiences and explained how unfair societal gender norms and cultural practices result in stigma and discrimination explicitly experienced by widowed women in rural areas.

Applying an intersectional lens to the interview discussions combined with a focus on women's experiences with regional location, ethnicity, age, and socio-economic differences opened up new conversations about participants' personal experiences with gender inequality. In so doing, however, the partner organization staff often framed their discussion from an 'externalizing' lens towards gender inequality as something "out there" in other communities rather than experiences that impact women in their localities.

Another interview participant talked about working in some of the poorest provinces of Vietnam and noted that "gender issues are still big issues in far remote areas." Because of this, the work involved promoting women to help them get jobs in the tourism industry. The participant further explained: "women from ethnic minorities had to work very hard, they don't have equality at all in the family, because they are not independent in the family". However, as the interviewee noted, sustainable jobs are vital to accessing income for women who have few options for work. When job opportunities in tourism are created, women can improve their lives. The interviewee also noted that these efforts are important because gender inequality is slower to be realized in the countryside, and women are not treated as equal to men.

When revealed in the interviews, the examples of gender inequality as something 'out there' in other communities, created a starting point for further discussions about gender inequality more broadly defined. These conversations often turned to partner organization staff recognizing that the gender division of labor relates to their areas of work, with specific implications for gender relations and women's experiences of inequality, women's voice in decision making, and women's experiences of intersectional inequality. For example, discussions turned to the higher workload for women responsible for significant reproductive work and unpaid care work, leaving limited time for their career and income-earning activities, including developing a start-up business. For example, one respondent in Vietnam explained his knowledge of challenges for women in business as such: "There are some barriers for women in businesses. Many men want women to stay home and spend more time with the family, taking care of children, men and family members do not support women with business." Likewise, another female interviewee noted that "in my family, I also have a job with eight hours in office like my husband, but I still have to spend more time to take care of children and unnamed work."

In Tanzania, one participant highlighted what he saw as challenges to doing gender equality work with beneficiary communities since, as he described, an understanding of gender relations is different in the rural communities: "First of all, they [volunteers from the Global North] have to understand the Tanzanian context. I am sure where they come from, and Tanzania is two different things: you may find the issue of gender is quite different". This participant suggested requiring development organization staff "to sit with indigenous people and learn about our gender" before designing programming that may not otherwise reflect their cultural realities.

Other examples of partner organization staff reflecting on the nature of gender inequality in rural or remote areas could be found in comments provided by a Peruvian partner organization staff who mentioned the strategy required to design programs that address gender inequality when working in rural areas. This staff member was concerned because "you run the risk, as an NGO [that] wants to empower women, and in a community where there are more men – especially *machista* men, than women could close the door on you." The participant's concern was that community members would refuse to engage in programming that promotes women's equality if it is perceived to transgress gender norms in those communities.

4.3 Opportunities for Improved Gender Awareness in Transnational Spaces Through International Development Volunteering

Changing perspectives on the significance and relevance of gender equality as a development priority (both in the communities where organizations are working and within the organizations) have been facilitated, in part, by interactions with IDVs. Generally, IDVs were seen as bringing critical capacity-building skills in the area of gender equality programming. For example, according to staff in a Vietnamese partner organization, gender-related support from IDVs was needed because: "We are still struggling ourselves .... We don't have a gender training strategy or approach in a systematic way".

In support of the work of partner organizations, IDVs were also able to strengthen the day-to-day running of business operations through their communication and information technology skills, allowing for the intensification of host partner organizations' efforts towards GEWE. As a participant from Ghana noted:

Most of our international volunteers supported us to use social media to high-light the issue of women in our work. So there [have] been instances where we used that as a model and the involvement of the international volunteers and their expertise in ICT [information communication technology] helped us to improve our work.

At the organizational level, IDVs were valued for their fresh perspectives. As a participant from Tanzania said:

What I value the most is [their] experience and perception of things. People are coming from various environments, which is a very good thing for us. We need very fresh eyes on some old stuff so that we can modify or do them better. They say, if you are doing something for a very long time, you might develop, or you can grow monotony. Fresh eyes help us develop.

As transnational actors, IDVs also brought new perspectives and created new opportunities that were needed to change attitudes. For example, in Vietnam, volunteers brought about different perspectives to address the problem of gender inequality from various angles: "Having someone from outside the region with different perspectives, especially on gender, gave the participants a different way of understanding the issues at the global scale."

Other partner organization staff talked about improved work in the area of gender equality as a result of partnering with IDVs. For example, as a participant from Ghana noted, the IDVs reinforced the value and significance of a gender focus in working with small-holder farmers and helped include more women in these projects. The IDVs were also instrumental in enhancing the skills and competencies of organization staff through their contributions to training. For example, in Ghana, the participant noted:

The international volunteers insist we make sure that [the training] is gender-sensitive such that it won't be all male or all female. Because of that, we try to bring both sexes to make sure that responsibilities are given to people, not because of their gender but to ensure that everybody in the organization has a role to play.

Other contributions provided by IDVs to organizational gender mainstreaming efforts included work to create gender policies within the organization. For example, in Uganda, IDVs provided support in relation to sexual harassment policies. They shared their experiences and knowledge from their own countries to help local universities in Uganda to develop a sexual harassment policy. A Ugandan participant expressed their appreciation for the IDVs who provided support that enabled them to incorporate gender equality into their programming. In another example, IDVs in Senegal assisted with various activities involving "gender strategizing" that helped organization staff build their capacities in gender equality programming. They also helped develop legal instruments and gender training that helped facilitate capacity building among member organizations. Finally, in Nepal, the IDVs played a role in creating action plans that helped the organization "increase the number of female members in the cooperatives, to include women in the policy and decision-making level."

Many of these changes were directly attributed to the intervention of IDVs. For example, according to a staff member in Nepal, it was "only after the arrival of the … volunteer [that] we realized the need, and importance of, GESI [Gender Equality and Social Inclusion] in [our] organization". Another participant in Malawi reinforced the distinctive contributions made by IDVs to their programs and policies: "I can proudly say that we have what we call a gender policy, [and] it is because of the initiative from the same volunteers."

In addition to these benefits, participants also identified several challenges or areas for further consideration. These suggestions were provided to help organizations get the best support possible through transnational interactions. One example of room for improvement was the level of expertise and professional experience that IDVs could bring. Most organizations required staff with gender expertise who could provide them with technical skills and advice on gender mainstreaming and women's empowerment. However, many IDVs had not been sufficiently trained on this issue. Some partner organizations were frustrated with the lack of formal training in gender equality programming among the IDVs, especially considering the organization's need for this professional support and technical skills in gender mainstreaming. As one participant from Vietnam noted: "For the volunteers coming here, I don't think they had enough gender training or specific gender skills to help us to do gender activities. It would be useful to have a gender advisor to support us". Recognizing these challenges improved training among IDVs was considered highly valuable.

Participants noted that partner organizations could play a more prominent role in screening applicants to ensure that IDVs came to their communities with the technical skills needed to support gender mainstreaming in the community organizations. They suggested that doing so would require better communication between the volunteer sending organizations and the partner organizations. As a participant from Guatemala noted: "[...] it would be better to have more communication between us – because we never know what is going on in the process until out of nowhere, they have a volunteer for us. It would be better to have more communication."

Other areas for consideration were the increased amount of time provided by the IDVs and closer attention to gaps created in the timing of their departure from the organization. There was a lack of continuity after volunteers left because partner organizations did not have enough personnel to fill the full-time positions required for the projects started by volunteers. As a result, the two-way flow of knowledge necessary to facilitate capacity building and long-term sustainability was negatively impacted by the limited window for integration into the community. In Ghana, a respondent felt that with the complexity of GEWE:

> *The duration of the volunteers is short. It is barely 11 months. For me, that is not enough for the volunteers to actually understand the culture and make any serious impact when it comes to gender equality and women empowerment. Gender issues are very critical issues; you do not empower women overnight; one year is very short.*

Many respondents agreed that a limited duration negatively impacted the effectiveness of IDVs' integration into the community and thus their impacts on GEWE initiatives. As a result, the two-way flow of knowledge necessary to facilitate capacity building and long-term sustainability was negatively impacted by the limited time window for IDVs' integration into the community.

Although IDVs and volunteer programs contributed to promoting GEWE in many countries, many challenges need to be tackled to ensure the success of volunteer programs and the meaningful contribution of IDVs. Respondents expressed their frustrations with expertise and professional experience on GEWE, as many volunteers lacked formal training in gender equality work. On the other hand, while many IDVs lacked professional experience in gender equality, most were viewed as flexible and willing to learn how to assist with GEWE initiatives. Increased communications with partner organizations during the recruitment process could address this gap. In summary, IDVs' level of expertise, cultural adaptability and sensitivity; time spent in the role/country; and language barriers were frequently identified as major factors that impeded GEWE outcomes.

5. Analysis

Despite international and national commitments to gender mainstreaming and prioritizing gender equality as a cross-cutting theme, development organizations face several challenges and barriers to effectively operationalizing gender equality commitments. The findings documented in this paper reveal the challenges of gender mainstreaming, including resistance to gender equality priorities, despite national commitments to international gender equality priorities.

Resistance to discussions about gender inequality is not new and is an inevitable response to social change (Flood et al. 2020). These findings reinforce various forms of resistance to gender equality and gender mainstreaming articulated in previous scholarships, such as denial of the problem, refusal to recognize responsibility to address issues, inaction to implement a change, and the use of violence and harassment (Flood et al. 2020; Moser/Moser 2005). In the paper, one of the most common forms of resistance is a perceived preferential treatment accorded to women with examples of international women's day events, programs that prioritize women and girls, and assumptions about gender equality based on existing gender norms. Problematically, however, these perceived preferences were provided without consideration for patriarchal structures that could quickly negate many of these perceived advantages.

Additional examples of resistance to gender mainstreaming were observed in relation to the simplistic approach to reporting on gender equality outcomes in project reporting. Partner organizations generally employed a Women in Development (WID) approach or liberal feminist approach that counted women participants as the basis of their evidence of gender equality work. While including women in program activities is an important starting point for addressing gender inequality, it is also insufficient for tackling the structural causes of marginalization or oppression that many women experience (Cornwall 2003). For many organizations, counting the number of women participants was seen as an effective and sufficient strategy for monitoring and evaluating gender equality results and impacts. However, this simple measure ultimately tells us little about gender equality outcomes. It is insufficient to assume that "if more are counted, they'll count more" (Nelson 2015: 41).

The simple measures of counting women participants are employed at the expense of capturing fuller, thicker understandings of gender inequality which expose the structures and institutions that perpetuate inequality and masculinist societal norms. Other important questions remain, including questions about whether women participants' voices are heard, whether decisions made by women are legitimized by men in the community, and whether differences between diverse women are considered in decision-making processes. Therefore, it is also vital to examine how gender equality initiatives help to challenge gender stereotypes and the structural causes of inequality, the unequal relations between men and women, and the intersectional realities of diverse members of a community. Just as "development is intrinsically about power" (Radcliffe 2015: 855), so too is gender equality about tackling the inequitable power relations that perpetuate women's oppression. Gathering this richer data (beyond the mere counting of women participants) would help expose women's experiences as they navigate social and institutional manifestations of inequality (Hay 2012) and their agency as they seek to change the structures that contribute to their marginalization.

The findings also uncovered specific examples of how gender inequality is understood by organizational staff. Specifically, beyond the resistance to address gender issues within the organization (in policies, practices, and monitoring, evaluating, and reporting activities), partner organizations noted some opportunities for considering gender inequality. However, those spaces for tackling gender inequality were primarily viewed as issues considered external to the organization or a problem to be solved elsewhere in the communities or rural areas where programs are delivered. When partner organizations were asked for more information about why gender inequality is a consideration for their programmatic work, staff members often turned to an intersectional analysis, documenting the experiences of specific groups of women such as widows or women who have very little income. In so doing, partner organizations rejected essentialisms of women's experiences and highlighted intersecting realities of oppression and inequality faced by particular groups of women. These intersectional analyses are important for understanding the unique and specific issues faced by diverse members of the community, highlighting discrimination based on age, marital status, ethnicity, education levels, socio-economic status, etc. These insights lend themselves to transformative gender mainstreaming (Parpart 2014) and can be used as examples for expanding gender mainstreaming initiatives. In addition to this more nuanced understanding of intersectional gender issues, partner organizations must also consider how gender inequality is experienced in all communities and within the organizations themselves. The assumption that gender inequality is solely an issue for the "beneficiary communities" results in few opportunities for organizational staff to consider how diverse experiences of gender inequality affect their own lives and the lives of others within their organizations.

Partner organizations see IDVs as valuable transnational actors who offer insights into gender equality strategies to be applied both within the organization and in the organization's programmatic work in the communities where they work. Several examples were provided by partner organizations of how IDVs were able to introduce gender mainstreaming activities to expose gender inequality within the organization. IDVs also helped improve exposure to new ideas and introduced policies, training, and capacity building in gender equality. In so doing, IDVs were seen as transforming gender relations through everyday interactions, by building confidence in GEWE programming, and by modeling behavior that fosters changes in gender norms (Tiessen/Rao/Lough 2020). Broadened perspectives on GEWE began with increased intercultural exposure between IDVs and staff members. IDVs, therefore, play an essential role in shaping how partner organizations understand power dynamics, gender relations, and root causes of inequality.

Perhaps most importantly, many of the findings highlighted challenges that need to be addressed by organizations involved in sending volunteers abroad. Volunteer-sending organizations need to pay careful attention to strengthening IDVs' level of expertise and capacity to lead gender equality training, as well as their cultural adaptability and sensitivity. The expertise that IDVs can bring to partner organizations for more effective and transformative gender mainstreaming impacts includes additional support for administrative, financial, human resources management.

Other support that IDVs could provide includes help with changing organizational procedures, facilitating the creation of organizational gender equality policies, and supporting programs and training to create changes in staff attitudes and behaviors (Tiessen 2007). Additional support that IDVs can bring to partner organization staff includes great attention to gender equality strategies beyond counting the number of women and men participants. This might involve researching the gender-specific needs of participants (such as childcare or travel-related needs that are impacted by the gender division of labor within the household). Monitoring and evaluation strategies can be enhanced through IDV support by delving deeper into gender relations and the underlying reasons for women's lack of participation in programs or the barriers to women's success in projects.

6. Conclusion

This paper examines some of the challenges of mainstreaming gender equality in partner organizations, with examples of resistance, externalizing gender problems as specific to 'beneficiary communities' rather than the organizations themselves, and, in some instances, the limited impact IDVs have on promoting gender-sensitive programming. Several challenges to gender mainstreaming were provided by partner organizations interviewed for this study.

Addressing these challenges requires strategic efforts to work with partner organization staff to uncover gender inequality perpetuating within and by the organization. Doing so will facilitate a more comprehensive approach to gender mainstreaming that focuses on the organizational practices, policies, procedures, monitoring, evaluating, and reporting on gender-related work.

Opportunities for development organizations to look inward to their practices and organizational cultures can help partner organization staff reflect on the subtle and overt ways gender inequality is reproduced in day-to-day operation and acts of discrimination. They can also reveal the attitudes and behaviors that prevent changes needed to support gender equality. Uncovering these barriers within the organization is an important first step to understanding the obstacles to promoting gender equality in the communities where projects are implemented. Exposing the resistance to discussions of gender equality within partner organizations is a first step to recognizing the spaces where gender equality programs and interventions are needed. IDVs can play a valuable role in helping partner organization staff uncover some of the resistances to considering gender equality in the organization's day-to-day operations. IDVs bring fresh insights and outside perspectives that are valued by partner organization staff. These perspectives can be central to starting conversations about institutionalized gender inequalities within the organizations.

Throughout the interviews, attention to diverse forms of resistance to gender equality programming uncovered perceptions among some participants that gender equality programming favors women and can be seen to leave men and boys behind. Thus, addressing gender relations is central to effective gender equality programming, and IDVs can play an important role in the training and information sharing that explains gender inequality effectively to prevent misunderstandings.

The findings presented in this paper also revealed that gender inequality is generally observed as a problem to be tackled elsewhere and often, according to the partner organization staff, in the rural communities where projects are implemented. Recognizing gender inequality in these communities is a valuable starting point for considering some of the causes and consequences of discrimination or oppression of marginalized groups. As the participants noted, it is insufficient to view women as a cohesive group with the same experiences or challenges. Throughout the interviews, participants highlighted specific examples of intersecting factors that contributed to power imbalances, stigma, or diverse forms of disadvantage among women with specific lived experiences (specifically women who become widows, who are low income, or who have an excessive workload that prevents them from actively participating in project activities).

IDVs were generally considered valuable contributors to the organizations as they provide an essential role in supporting organizations in ways that allow them to integrate gender equality into a range of policies and practices that helped the organizations improve sex and gender-disaggregated data, enhanced training and capacity building, and improved policy and procedural approaches. IDVs also played an essential role in promoting gender equality and women's empowerment by providing new perspectives on gender issues and strategies to address gender inequality across various programs. Ensuring that IDVs come with gender equality expertise is crucial for supporting partner organization staff identified as priorities for improving their gender mainstreaming efforts. IDVs can therefore be an important contributor to gender mainstreaming within the organization and in the organization's programs. In order for IDVs to be more effective, the partner organizations highlighted the need for IDVs to come with a clear understanding of gender mainstreaming tools and strategies and knowledge of gender equality programming.

Bibliography

Cornwall, Andrea (2003): Whose voices? Whose choices? Reflections on gender and participatory development. In: World Development, vol. 31, no. 8, pp. 1325-1342.

Derbyshire, Helen (2002): Gender Manual. A practical guide for development policymakers and practitioners. London, https://www.rcrc-resilience-southeastasia.org/wp-content/uploads/2015/12/gendermanual.pdf (28.10.2021).

EIGE (2016): institutional transformation. Gender Mainstreaming Toolkit. https://eige.europa.eu/gender-mainstreaming/toolkits/gender-institutional-transformation (23.6.2021).

Flood, Michael; Dragiewicz, Molly; Pease, Bob (2020): Resistance and backlash to gender equality. In: Aust J Soc Issues, pp. 1-16.

Hay, Katherine (2012): Engendering Policies and Programmes through Feminist Evaluation. Opportunities and Insights. In: Indian Journal of Gender Studies, vol. 19, no. 2, pp. 321–340.

Jahan, Rounaq (1995): The Ilusive Agenda. Mainstreaming Women in Development. London.

Mannel, Jeneviève (2010): Gender mainstreaming Practice. Considerations for HIV/AID community organizations. In: AIDS care, vol. 22, no. 2, pp. 1613-1619.

Moser, Caroline; Moser, Annalise (2005): Gender Mainstreaming since Beijing. A review of success and limitations in international institutions. In: Gender and Development, vol. 13, no. 2, pp. 11-22.

Nelson, Diane M. (2015): Who Counts? the Mathematics of Death and Life after Genocide. Durham.

Parpart, Jane L. (2014): Exploring the transformative potential of gender mainstreaming in international development institutions. In: Journal of International Development, vol. 26, no. 3, pp. 382-395.

Radcliffe, Sarah A. (2015): Development Alternatives. In: Development and Change, vol. 46, no. 4, pp. 855-874.

Rao, Aruna; Sandler, Joanne; Kelleher, David; Miller, Carol (2016): Gender at work. Theory and practice for 21st Century Organizations. Abington.

Tiessen, Rebecca (2007): Everywhere/Nowhere. Gender mainstreaming in development agencies. Bloomfield.

Tiessen, Rebecca (2019): What's New About Canada's Feminist International Assistance Policy and Why' More of the Same' Matters. https://journalhosting.ucalgary.ca/index.php/sppp/article/view/MD%20-%2015 (4.6.2021).

Tiessen, Rebecca; Rao, Sheila; Lough, Benjamin J. (2020): International Development Volunteering as Transformational Feminist Practice for Gender equality. In: Journal of Developing Societies, vol. 37, no. 1, pp. 30-56.

UN Women (N.D.): Gender Mainstreaming. www.unwomen.org/-/media/headquarters/attachments/sections/library/publications/2020/gender-mainstreaming-strategy-for-achieving-gender-equality-and-empowerment-of-women-girls-en.pdf?la=en&vs=3849 (28.10.2021).

Valk, Minke (2000): An introduction: commitments to women and gender. In: Sarah, Cummings

Dam, Henk Van (ed.): Institutionalising gender equality: Commitment, policy, and Practice – A Global Sourcebook (Gender, Society & Development). Oxford.

Van Eerdewijk, Anouka; Davids, Tine (2014): Escaping the Mythical Beast. Gender Mainstreaming Reconceptualized. In: Journal of International Development, vol. 26, no. 3, pp. 303-316, DOI: 10.1002/jid.2947.

Vu, Vi (2017): Why women should ditch Women's Day. Retrieved from VN Express. https://e.vnexpress.net/news/perspectives/why-women-should-ditch-women-s-day-3551008.html (17.10.2021).

Wallace, Tina (1998): Institutionalising gender in UK NGOs. In: Development in Practice, vol. 8, no, 2, pp. 159-172.

Strings Attached? How Global South Partner Organizations' Perceptions of Feminism Shape their Relationships with Feminist Foreign Policy Donors from the Global North

Tiffany Laursen

1. Introduction

As part of a larger global movement to promote gender equality and women's empowerment (GEWE), governments have increasingly tied their bilateral foreign aid agendas to feminist foreign policy (FFP). In 2014, Sweden was the first country to proclaim that its bilateral foreign aid policies would promote feminist ideals. In 2017, Canada announced its Feminist International Assistance Program (FIAP) would focus on eradicating poverty through promoting shared values by committing no less than 95 percent of Canada's bilateral international development assistance would "target or integrate gender equality and the empowerment of women and girls" by 2021-2022 (Global Affairs Canada 2017). More recently, France, Mexico, and Spain have committed to FFP while the United Kingdom and Australia have revamped their focus to align with FFP. Moreover, Iceland, Ireland, Belgium, and the Netherlands have committed more than 60 percent of aid to FFP/ GEWE without a formal declaration (OECD 2018).

Although a welcomed commitment to advancing equality and opportunities for women and girls, some critics claim that FFPs (particularly FIAP) contain vague goals and outcomes (Morton/Muchiri/Swiss 2020) while instrumentalizing women and girls (Tiessen 2019). Further, they proclaim the need to utilize more innovative approaches when translating policy into action (Rao/Tiessen 2020). Other critiques warn of the importance of understanding the plight of women and girls in their context without importing western ideals (Robinson 2021) while also considering the diverse views and locally-based approaches to feminism (Rao/ Tiessen 2020). The cautionary advice recognizes the history of the various forms of feminism originating in the Global South. In Africa, for example, Mama (2004) identifies the roots of feminism trace back to the 18th century (and potentially earlier), while more modern approaches based their activism on an African agenda set in 1977 by the founding of the Association of African Women for Research and Development (Ampofo et al. 2004). More broadly, Global South feminist activism has largely coincided with political public discourse around post-independence nation building and globalization (Mohanty 1984; Ampofo et al. 2004). National movements shaped the way feminists in Africa and Asia framed their discussion points away from domestic violence and reproductive rights opting instead to center their advocacy on "militarism and health, to environmental and economic justice, social development, human rights, and population" (Antrobus 1996: 64).

Another aspect of Global South feminist advocacy was the erasure of "global sisterhood" which asserted women's oppression was solely related to the commonality of their gender. Theorists instead offered intersectionality as a guiding lens for development programming, which recognizes compounding effects of multiple variables including class, race, and ethnicity (among others) in the struggle to obtain social justice for women (Mohanty 1984; Antrobus 1996). Intersectionality includes diverse perspectives that are reflective of a variety of local contexts. Without recognizing the variations and contextually relevant voices, one risks assuming that all women – particularly all women in the Global South – have the same interests, challenges, and agendas (Mohanty 1984; Win 2004; Okech/Musindarwezo 2019). Narayanaswamy (2016) takes this one step further by explaining that even the more recent effort to create spaces for less dominant voices from the Global South is limited by the small representation of Southern feminist voices and the narrowly defined conception of feminism, joining the call for a greater emphasis on locally-based feminisms (Moghadam 1998).

To more fully include the multiplicity of voices and perspectives of diverse feminisms rising from the Global South, there requires a rejection of a hierarchal ranking of dominant forms of feminism (often associated with Western feminism), and an inclusion of more peripheral interpretations of feminisms (Lal et al. 2010). Decentering Western feminism and embracing diverse feminisms paints a more accurate picture of local agency whereby the wide array of Southern voices are viewed as "fully capable of accurately interpreting their complex reality, rather than [Northern scholars] attempting to represent their perspectives on their behalf" (Tiessen/Lough/Cheung 2012: 138). This guarantees feminist knowledge is not only reflective of the numerous backgrounds displaying diverse voices, but also allows the re-centering of knowledge to include the voices in the various regions of the Global South. Bringing in the voices of people who have otherwise been overlooked or silenced is not only necessary but also invaluable in guaranteeing the efficiency and positive influence of FFP on livelihoods.

2. Literature Review: Links between Policy, Funding, and Implementation

The framing of feminist agency becomes a pivotal intersection for FFP and GEWE initiatives laying between public policy (e.g., FIAP, Sweden's feminist foreign policy), NGO funding initiatives, and transnational actors including international development volunteers and partner organizations in the Global South. In this juncture there is an ongoing process of negotiations, where the values and priorities of multiple stakeholders come together to make decisions on program funding and thereby development. Theorizing relationships between NGOs and governments, Coston (1998) describes a continuum between asymmetrical power based on resistance to pluralism (isomorphism and dependence) characterized in three ways (repression, rivalry, and competition), and symmetrical power based on acceptance of pluralism characterized in five ways (contracting, third party, cooperation, complementarity, collaboration). Simply, organizations will push against donor-imposed initiatives to varying degrees as they strategically navigate their social mission objectives. Empirical analysis show many Global South organizations conform while some are able to resist donor agendas (Rauh 2010; Lefroy/ Tsarenko 2013). Moreover, promoting local initiatives through network support requires rethinking "the link between policy and implementation, recognizing that both are political processes and that while policies set agendas, both policies and their implementation are deeply influenced by societal factors" (Parpart 2014: 382). While FFP agendas and GEWE programs are largely shaped by societal factors, the norms and values that shape the application of feminist ideology between donors in the Global North and implementers in the Global South may vary significantly.

Sundstrom (2005: 422) expands this argument to consider the way foreign aid is used to promote universal norms and the limited impact these universal norms have on a "successful NGO movement."

To add to this framework, it is important to move beyond the binary of "conformity" and "resistance" to consider the process of negotiation, partial adaption, and diplomacy. Building on this analytical lens, this paper draws on interview data from ten countries in the Global South. This paper explores Global South partner organization's perspectives on how the emergence of FFP from the Global North has shaped their relationships with donors as well as the programs that support local beneficiaries. Exploring how FFPs play out in practice, several questions guide the analysis: are donor initiatives known to partners? Do Global South partner organizations integrate feminist priorities into their programs to obtain funding? Do donor approaches resonate with their own feminist/development priorities – why or why not? What is the perceived value added, if any, of FFP?

3. Methods

Interviews were conducted in 2018 – 2019 with 150 partner organization staff in ten countries. Once all interviews were transcribed, data were coded to identify common themes throughout. Data were analyzed using discourse analysis. The introduction to this special edition has more detailed information on the methodology for data collection and the analysis of findings.

4. Findings

The questions outlined above were examined in the interview transcripts using discourse analysis. Each of the scripts were open coded using Atlas.ti.9 software. The following themes emerged as predominately discussed among all interviews: variation in the level of awareness of FFP, variations in the level of utilization and integration of FFP, variation in perception of congruence between Global North donor agendas and Global South priorities, and the distinct contributions donor policies have made to GEWE. As each theme was explored, the overall findings reveal that partner organizations in the Global South pursue partnership-style relationships with NGOs in the Global North where autonomy and cultural relevancy are valued as organizations navigate FFP.

4.1 Awareness Levels of FFP/GEWE Tied to Donor Agendas

During interviews, partner organization staff were asked whether the donor policies guiding the work of their Global North NGOs partners were known to them. Particularly, partner organization staff were asked whether they had heard about FFP. Further, we inquired about how international feminist policies like FIAP are guiding development work in their country through specific channels such as Canadian NGO collaborations and the role and impact of transnational actors such as IDVs. The degree to which staff were aware of FFP ranged from those who have never heard of FFP to those who are well versed and actively implementing projects. Those who have never heard about FFP were aware of feminism more broadly: "We have not heard about the policy in Sweden or Canada, but we are aware about the feminist perspective and how it works in general" (Nepal). Some were unaware of policies because they had not investigated it: "No. I could have heard, but it's not something I really dig into" (Tanzania).

Several interviewees commented on their knowledge of FFP but were unaware of the particulars, such as in Ghana: "Not the details of them but I do know the existence." Moreover, some interviewees tied their limited knowledge to having GEWE in their periphery resulting in lack of awareness, as in Vietnam: "I heard a bit about that, but I didn't really do a lot of research... We have been running a few projects on gender equality promotion, but it doesn't mean that we are very strong in women's issues." Still, others were aware and have studied FFP, like in Uganda: "I've read about them...They have a document about international relations in respect to gender." Still, others were aware because they are required to report outcomes: "We are familiar because it [is] something we have to show on the proposals" (Tanzania).

4.2 Utilization Levels

Corresponding to level of awareness, utilization of FFP funding ranged between those who do not utilize it in any way and those who do. Those who do not utilize the donor initiatives noted their reasoning was based on either their lack of knowledge of opportunities or their reliance on other sources of income: "We do not receive the budget from the government, we are funded by products and services" (Vietnam). However, several partner organization staff stated their level of utilization is tied to the organization remaining autonomous: "Decisions need to be made by us. We are happy to talk about things, but ultimately, we make the decisions about what we think is best for us" (Guatemala).

Several study participants presented examples of not applying for funding because of the inability to meet donor's requirements. This was largely a concern when donors required quotas for a specific number or percent of women to be involved in the implementing organization: "We couldn't even apply for that funding because one of the requirements was that at least 50% of the leadership of the organization should be women, and ours was 40%" (Tanzania). Partner organizations also discussed the requirements for women's participation in organizational leadership positions: "We were looking for a communications person and wanted a woman. It was very difficult; we couldn't reach our goals. Sometimes, when you come to the effectiveness and efficiency, it's not easy to get [70 percent women]" (Tanzania).

In their quest to build capacity, another frustration came from requiring female-led initiatives when women were not trained first. Interviewees from Malawi elaborated on this point noting that women need training to be equipped to take on leadership roles. The interviewee described examples of donors funding women-only projects that resulted in unsuccessful programs because the women were "not well qualified to handle the project."

Funding tied to women in organizational leadership was seen as having potential for opportunities if donors are willing to be flexible. A participant from Tanzania noted the significance of flexibility in funding arrangements so they can more effectively use the resources to "improve the gender relations in our organization, but also to improve the capacity of women to take more responsibilities throughout the organization." The participant went on to explain that without flexibility in the funding model, the organization is unable to build the capacity of the women to implement the project.

Other interviewees took this sentiment a bit further. They described a negotiation process weighing the interests between donor objectives and project outcomes that involved strategies to get women into leadership positions. This negotiation process fills priorities for both donors and the organization "when we post a woman from that level to higher level, we fulfill the donor's interests. But we finish with our interests by getting women and men on the common ground" (Tanzania).

Out of these requirements for GEWE targets, some partner organizations expressed that their priorities have to be adapted to survive: "The world has changed and most of the organization or countries are focusing on providing more knowledge to women and youth. Without the organization shifting, it's going to be very difficult for an organization to be stable" (Tanzania). One interviewee suggested shifting requirements away from organizations and towards the beneficiaries, thereby building capacity for future leaders: "If we empower girls [beneficiaries of our services], then we will be able, later, to get them into leadership. But…if the policies don't target the beneficiaries, then you won't reach this 50/50 in decision making" (Tanzania).

Even if partner organization staff were unsure of their capacity to meet donor requirements, some have taken up the challenge and applied for funding. They used the opportunity to assess their situation prior to accepting investment, particularly when the money has been tied to increasing the number of women participating in projects as in Tanzania: "We had one week …to start planning, to [send] information, so [we could] get [minimum of 60% women] …to attend that workshop. We did that and we saw it was something we can now manage…So we accepted the proposal" (Tanzania). (See Nguyen's article in this collection for further discussion on mainstreaming gender priorities).

Given their utilization strategies, partner organizations found ways to incorporate gender requirements into their programming as described by an interviewee in Ghana: "If you are doing training, for instance, then you have to figure a way out to add gender equality component to it for it to qualify for funding… to receive funding from FIAP." However, it appears that much of the interpretation of donor requirements involved increasing the number of women participating. Still, some organizations do not just pad their training with increased number of women to obtain funding; they are actively engaging and promoting initiatives: "Thanks to these policies from other countries, we've gotten funding for organizations to protect women and I think this has improved a lot" (Guatemala). The improvement (interpreted as stemming from Canada's FIAP) was noted as a welcomed change for women, as one Ghanaian interviewee illuminated: "Women have always been on the wrong side of things for years so there's nothing wrong with [trying to] balance the equation."

4.3 Perceptions of Coherence of FFP/GEWE Between Donors and Partner Organizations

Beyond understanding levels of awareness and utilization, we were also interested to know the level of similarity between partner organizations and donors' perceptions of feminism, FFP, and GEWE. We specifically asked if FFP has changed the way services are planned and provided to the beneficiaries. Some interviewees expressed concerns with donors that attach strings to their initiatives because GEWE initiatives left men and boys out of capacity building "…when a feminist is leading this type of work, they insist on the feminist approach and then they leave out the men…" (Malawi). Specific examples from Malawi demonstrate the need for a broader approach to community development that promises buy-in from all members of the community. This should particularly include men and boys since they can act as the 'gatekeepers' and limit or reverse program success. In their experience, GEWE programming targeting only women and girls results in spoken and unspoken backlash. One interviewee described a scenario where micro finance programs designed solely for women failed to gain buy in from men who in turn "are the ones [that] are going to frustrate these kinds of efforts." This interviewee further described a sabotaging effect in a scenario where girls were given scholarships for secondary education, but when the community was surveyed, the organization found that instances of early pregnancy rose while instances of dropping out of school had not changed. Upon inquiring, the communities expressed that some of the boys were poorer than the girls who received scholarship. In turn, the boys got frustrated and focused on disrupting girls' education. The interviewee concluded with one important, albeit hard learned, lesson: "If you don't build capacities in families and communities to handle these issues even if you finance these initiatives, sometimes they don't yield the results you expected because Malawi is not Sweden, Malawi is not Canada." (See Shahadu Bitamsimli's article in this collection for further discussion on including men and boys).

An adapted strategy between donor initiatives and community objectives was raised in a conversation about how to tackle root causes of gender inequality. A Nepalese interviewee explained the relationship between economic status and domination as a primary root cause of gender inequality: "If we cannot provide access to resources and information, then this situation cannot be changed by lobbying and advocacy…If …you have access to resources, nobody can dominate you. Whether you are female or part of another socially excluded group."

In accordance with addressing root causes of inequality, it appears there is a perception that donors lack understanding the reality of country contexts. Some interviewees suggested that donors have vague end goals that they struggle to tie to community objectives. The struggle for donor relevancy was perceived by some partner organization staff to stem from inadequate vetting as donors post requests for proposals and then evaluate writing skills as opposed to building relationships with partners who are intermediaries to the beneficiaries: "A best writer is not the right partner... Donors should change their modality; they should approach the partner directly. They should build capacity of the partner, but also go directly to meet the beneficiaries through the partners..." (Tanzania).

Staff from partner organizations considered the misunderstandings between themselves and donors explaining that donors were "not informed... every donor needs to know more" (Tanzania). Moreover, interviewees used the perceived disconnect to invite donors to their communities: "They should come on the ground [and ask], 'what do you need? What do you need for the coming year? What do you need from me?" (Tanzania). This approach to assessing needs would begin to address misunderstandings.

In a striking critique of the disconnect between cultural context and donor understanding, a broad concern emerged that contingency aid takes advantage of beneficiaries. One Malawian interviewee expressed: "Attaching such kind of conditions to aid I feel [is] just taking advantage of the poverty that people have. People are poor and we should not attach conditions to assisting the poor." Seemingly tied to this ideology (and that of the concerns raised above) was an overwhelming reiteration that organizations will not accept financial assistance that does not align to their objectives – appearing to solidify the autonomy of partner organizations: "If we were to accept [funding] then it means that it aligns with what we are already thinking or the policies that exist in this country" (Ghana).

In this alignment, many interviewees expressed their commitment to global causes including GEWE – sometimes expressing their own expertise. In Senegal for instance, one participant stated, "we specialize on these issues. We have our terminology that does not differ too much from what is being done at the global level." Further, many partner organization staff expressed that FFP is helpful to their initiatives "even before you ask whether we shall align, we are already aligned and as such any other organization that will come in to fund such a program will just be enhancing a lot of value and improving human dignity" (Kenya). Beyond alignment, organizations expressed their guiding principles are not negotiable and are the bedrock of their organizational permanence: "If we were not able to follow the policy, we have created for ourselves, we would be nothing." (Tanzania). Another interviewee in Tanzania asserted, "because we are not against [GEWE]... your support cannot really dismantle our framework... We will not allow that. But we don't show it, we persuade them."

Calculated decision-making seemed to be a strategic undertone. One Guatemalan interviewee described 'collaborative wins,' seeking funding that is a "win-win situation for us. For example, a Guatemalan congresswoman wanted to give us funding recently, and it was going to be good money, but the things that she wanted to do were not worth the money."

Beyond mutual wins, interviewees described a vetting process. The process reflected careful decision making that challenges the notion that civil society organizations (particularly in the Global South) will desperately accept funding regardless of goal alignment. Instead, as exemplified by a Tanzanian interviewee, the vetting process starts with understanding criteria, thematic areas, and how the funding objectives are in line with their work in the communities: "Before writing a proposal ...we consider...three things: the demand of the community, the demand of donor, but also the demand of the government by using existing policies, strategies, plans, laws... to ensure that [every component] ...complements each another."

To summarize, many interviewees did not believe that donor policies changed the work they did largely because: "Our mission is already deeply rooted in women's... empowerment" (Guatemala). Moreover, interviewees asserted selection bias when discussing their strategic responses to donor calls for proposals: "We don't respond to every call, but we fix to our mission and objective of the organization" (Tanzania). Selection bias gives further evidence that organizations in this sample are autonomous entities, free of dependency. Emerging from the data are an abundant amount of evidence that interviewees possess an embedded sense of ownership over their own initiatives:

The funding that are being delivered from outside must meet our demands. The original idea must be borne by us...developed by us and what we believe in. Imposing an external influence... we honestly don't entertain that... We existed for more than 6 years without external support (Tanzania).

In conjunction with importance of local ownership, interviewees provided strong evidence that context matters. A large concern was FFP originating in the Global North does not translate well when applied to Global South countries. As a Ghanaian woman proclaimed: "I am an African. And African women – our cultural background is different than somebody from Sweden." Another Ghanaian interviewee clarified: "Development support that requires us to adjust into feminist policies that are not in sync with our culture or that we find that doesn't bring in positive benefits to us is something that we will contest strongly" (Ghana). Interviewees provided examples of nuanced differences that effect programming – even within communities that are part of one country. In Tanzania, for example, an organization attempted a women's empowerment project with keeping chickens. However, in the local tribe, women were not permitted to have chickens resulting in failure: "When I came to encourage them or tell them to keep the chicken, it was difficult [for them] to understand my idea."

Beyond nuances, a larger discussion of context surrounded the legal translation of FFP, specifically when discussing LGBTQ+ and abortion rights. In countries where LGBTQ+ and abortion are illegal, some organizations expressed their decision to honor the legal system in their country for their own organizational survival: "LGTB is illegal... it can be a personal trait which we don't have any problem with, but we as an organization we have to follow the government regulations. If we go against it, it can be a disaster" (Tanzania). While some organizations honored laws, others found ways to navigate and/or compromise their practice to promote ideals like in Senegal where abortion is illegal: "Because of a strong lobby, we cannot work openly on [abortion], but must find strategies to strike a balance... with all the consequences resulting from women being raped, or who are subjected to incest and become pregnant...we look for solutions." In this compromise, however, organizations expressed that they risk not only legal repercussions but also future monetary support: "There are partners that finance you and then they hear that somewhere you are negotiating financing with people working on the issue of abortion, they can withdraw their financial support" (Senegal). In both examples, organizations strategically navigated their work, describing themselves as a liaison between donors and the communities they work. Interviewees confidently expressed their conviction that receiving money from a feminist-focused donor (such as FIAP) will not change their work because: "We work in the communities, so we know what is best for the communities and I believe we are in a better position to talk to any donor and see their terms and conditions." (Uganda)

Regardless of the limitations, partner organizations gave advice to their donors:

Whatever you do, if you're planning to implement an activity, [ask] what kind of legal management activities it has? For example, if you're doing economic empowerment, what are the policies in Tanzania that are dealing with economic empowerment? What are the policies, procedures, and administration on the ground are dealing with economic empowerment? What are the conventions, statements, and policies at the international level which are dealing with economic empowerment? How are they fitting up with your implementation at the local context? (Tanzania)

4.4 Unique Contributions of FFP/GEWE Donor Initiatives

Interviewees offered their observations about the unique contributions that FFPs have provided to programs. Several commented that donor initiatives force governments and organizations to think: "I think they push our country to think in different ways" (Guatemala). Another interviewee expressed: "When [the government] gets aid like that it forces the government to think...unless if they don't need the money then can say get your money and go out" (Malawi). In Uganda, an interviewee described receiving funds as an opportunity for growth: "I think it's an opportunity because if in our country we don't embrace feminism, I think they are going nowhere." The interviewee continued to describe their perception of the patriarchal society where male-dominated leadership makes decisions that maintain inequality through laws and limited funding. Moreover, this interviewee offered a solution: "If we had more women, things like more funds would be allocated to the education system and changing rules for girls to stay more in school."

Several interviewees described receiving money tied to GEWE as strengthening, maximizing, or enhancing their work and their global relationships: "[Receiving] funds [from] a government that has declared itself as feminist... strengthens us because it also improves the relationship" (Peru). In Kenya, an interviewee extended this notion by stating: "[Funding] such a program... [is bringing] a lot of value and improving human dignity and especially to the disadvantaged, to the most marginalized."

Overwhelmingly, interviewees described their relationships with donors as a strategic partnership: "We are not normally asking for help, but it is rather partnership and cooperation. We do plan together and do together" (Tanzania).

5. Analysis

The findings reveal the relationship between FFP, NGOs based in the Global North, and partner organizations based in the Global South consists of negotiations with important nuances in the management of competing priorities. Partner organizations highlight a range of responses to external funder priorities including acceptance, conciliation, compromise, resistance, and rejection. Decisions pertaining to partnerships with donors and implementing Global North NGOs (and the transnational actors that work in-between Global North NGOs and Global South partner organizations) reflect partner organization agency in decision-making, their strategies to navigate initiatives, as well as local priorities and cultural realities. Two common themes emerge from these findings: calculated decision making and discussion of shared values. This section considers these two findings and the distinct strategies employed to navigate these themes.

5.1 Calculated Decision Making

Admittedly, many of the interviewees in the sample are associated with feminist ideals, however, their candidness leads to a conclusion that while there are at times perceptions of imposed ideas/norms (be it from FFP originating in the West, or international development volunteers who bring their own culturally bound gender norms), partner organizations navigate, negotiate, and may ultimately resist forms of imposition. Their calculated decisions about the extent to which funding is needed and valued in relation to their own priorities, principles, and capacities is central to their strategic approaches. Partner organizations navigate structural inequalities while also exerting their own agency. For example, partner organization staff underscore the significant structural inequalities in which they must make decisions such as donor driven agendas. The example noted above pertaining to FFP being linked to program priorities has the potential to influence program commitments of partner organizations who are navigating systems of inequality with the purpose of addressing extreme poverty. Strategies identified by partners to mitigate or disrupt these structural inequalities were noted. Recommendations included increased commitment by donors to listen to local perspectives and inviting donors to visit the country and communities in which they live and work. Greater donor interaction is viewed as a pathway to fostering a stronger voice and improved partnership arrangement so that FFP initiatives better reflect local realities. The partnership-style approach allows for negotiating funding terms and is a strategic measure used to keep the interests of local governments, communities, and organizations at the center of initiatives. Improved relationships that allow and respect diverse perspectives between donors and partner organizations are instrumental in combatting Western imposed or donor-focused priorities. NGOs from the Global North that collaborate with partner organizations in the Global South could play a bigger role in advocating for increased donor responsiveness to local priorities. The mechanism to achieving this objective might involve the uniquely placed transnational actors working as IDVs. IDVs work closely with partner organizations and communities and through this sustained collaboration, observe the way that partner organizations navigate and translate FFP and GEWE priorities into relevant and accepted policy and practice within the partner country. IDVs can use this knowledge to inform – and to lend support to the voices of partner organizations in championing their priorities – to Global North NGOs and donors.

5.2 Discussion of Shared Values, Universal Norms, Local Manifestations, and Agency

Overwhelmingly, these data reinforce the significant ideal that 'context matters' in considering GEWE as a universally-shared value. The concept of universal norms and/or shared values is clear: people – regardless of culture – value and respect women and girls. The cultural context of GEWE, however, seems to be complicated with nuanced norms. Universally embraced norms may be that women are valued in societies, however, throughout the interviews it was clear that universal norms do not manifest themselves in all cultures the same way. Interviewees described the nuances in various examples: culture, laws, and LGBTQ+ rights; culture and funding girls' education and/or women's microenterprise at the expense of men and boys; creating spaces for women as professionals while also valuing and respecting the culturally coveted role as family nurturers (an interviewee explaining that Nepali women are given permission to leave work early to attend to family matters, for example). The position and status of women in society – including the way women experience respect, reverence, and subjugation – is more complex, nuanced, and related to context. The complexity stems from the nuances that are related to context (including law and culture which deserve separate description and analysis but expands beyond the scope of this paper) and is essential to the development and implementation of relevant GEWE programming. Local partner organizations with direct knowledge of these nuances strategically negotiate interests, attempting to find middle ground between donors' initiatives, beneficiary needs and cultural context, and local government laws and agendas. Although universal norms position organizations to accept funding, the nuanced differences create the spaces that open the door for negotiation. Partner organizations described continual negotiations with their donors to find common ground; therefore, the various manifestation of cultural values and the agile and diplomatic skill set of partner organization staff shape how FFPs play out in local contexts.

The variance in manifestations is where local culture and agency are central players in deconstructing local systems of oppression – as they see fit – which may differ from dominant perspectives, particularly those from the Global North. One example is the discussion on goals and outcomes. Scholarly critiques note that FIAP has vague goals (Morton/Muchiri/Swiss 2020), but interviewees in this study perceived donors' goals to be too focused. Staff from partner organizations expressed concerns that donor objectives that are too narrow may disqualify partner organizations from funding opportunities which could be used as a steppingstone to promote transformational change towards equality. The prominent example given was requiring a certain number of women to be in leadership positions to apply for funding. While vague goals hold organizations less accountable for specific outcomes, they also allow local initiatives more freedom to adapt programs that fit their local context and needs. Ambiguity may then provide time and space to train women appropriately and better position them for future success. In the example of promoting women to leadership, local manifestations could benefit from vague goals to obtain funding – fully recognizing that transformational gender equality requires more than counting the number of women in leadership positions. The onus would be on the partner organization to outline specific goals to train women for leadership – or a more locally relevant GEWE initiative – and to show the milestones for how the longer-term process of transformational change could occur. More generally and beyond the example of women in leadership (which admittedly is one small prong of a feminist approach which has a larger goal to promote transformational change), shouldn't the development field seek to allow donor funding that perhaps is fuzzier, but also petitions for context specific outcomes in projects that address local needs related to GEWE? Is that not the promise of accepting feminist multiplicity and embracing agency?

6. Conclusion

As Global North governments have increasingly tied their development aid to feminist foreign policy, Global South partner organizations have responded using many diverse strategies, (including, but not limited to, compromise and conciliation) while the recipient communities range in their response between acceptance and resistance to GEWE programming. The range of strategies utilized by partner organizations expand the conversation beyond Coston's (1998) discussion of push back by civil society organizations as well as Sundstrom's (2005) argument of promoting universal vs. local norms and impacts on NGO movements. Instead, partner organizations strategically navigate the funding mechanisms and priorities in relation to their ability to utilize funding in line with their own priorities, particularly when identifying community-level competencies and capacities to meet donor requirements. Many partner organizations welcome these opportunities, viewing them as openings for negotiating partnership style relationships. In this interaction, partner organizations in the Global South have maintained their autonomy and cultural relevancy, while also promoting GEWE initiatives in their countries – and specific cultural contexts. Greater flexibility among donors to allow local initiatives – and thus agency – to be at the center of development is central to recognizing locally-based feminisms. There may be a role for transnational actors such as IDVs working in-between the spaces of Global North NGOs and partner organizations who can better advocate for change at the policy level without compromising the autonomy and agency of partner organizations. As more countries and NGOs tie their funding to GEWE objectives, it is imperative to continue to "check in" with the level of autonomy partner organizations experience to maintain local relevancy, agency, and the expression of distinct and culturally specific feminisms.

Bibliography

Ampofo, Akosua Adomako; Beoku-Betts, Josephine; Ngaruiya Njambi, Wairimu; Osirim, Mary. (2004): Women's and gender studies in English-speaking sub-Saharan Africa. A review of research in the social sciences. In: Gender and Society, vol. 18, no. 6, pp. 685-714.

Antrobus, Peggy (1996): Bringing grassroots women's needs to the international arena. In: Development, vol. 39.

Coston, Jennifer (1998): A model and typology of government-NGO relationships. In: Nonprofit and Voluntary Sector Quarterly, vol. 27, no. 3, pp. 358-382.

Lal, Jayati; McCuire, Kristin; Stewart, Abigail J.; Zaborowska, Magdalena; Pas, Justine M. (2010): Recasting global feminisms: Toward a comparative historical approach to women's activism and feminist scholarship. In: Feminist Studies, vol. 36, no. 1, pp. 13-39.

Lefroy, Kathryn; Tsarenko, Yelena (2013): From receiving to achieving: The role of relationship and dependence for nonprofit organisations in corporate partnerships. In: European Journal of Marketing, vol. 47, no. 10, pp. 1641-1666.

Moghadam, Valentine M. (2002): Feminisms and Development. In: Gender & History, vol 10, no. 3, pp. 590-597.

Mama, Amina (2004): Demythologising gender in development: Feminist studies in African contexts. In: Institute of Development Studies Bulletin, vol. 35, no. 4, pp. 121-124.

Mohanty, Chandra Talpade (1984): Under Western eyes: Feminist scholarship and colonial discourses. In: Mohanty, Chandra Talpade; Russo, Ann; Torres, Lourdes (ed.): Third World Women and the Politics of Feminism. Bloomington, pp. 51-80.

Morton, Sam; Murchiri, Judyannet; Swiss, Liam (2020): Which feminism(s)? For Whom? Intersectionality in Canada's Feminist International Assistance Policy. In: International Journal, vol. 7, no. 3, pp. 329-348.

Narayanaswamy, Lata (2016): Whose feminism counts? Gender(ed) knowledge and professionalization in development. In: Third World Quarterly, vol. 37, no. 12, pp. 2156-2157.

OECD (2018): Aid to gender equality and women's empowerment: an overview. www.oecd. org/dac/gender-development (19.3.2021).

Okech, Awino; Musindarwezo, Dinah (2019): Transnational feminism and the Post-2015 Development Agenda. In: Soundings, vol. 71, pp. 75-90.

Parpart, Jane L. (2014): Exploring the transformative potential of gender mainstreaming in international development institutions. In: Journal of International Development, vol. 26, pp. 382-395.

Rao, Sheila; Tiessen, Rebecca (2020): Whose feminism(s)? Overseas partner organizations' perceptions of Canada's Feminist International Assistance Policy. In: International Journal, vol. 75, no. 3, pp. 349-366.

Rauh, Karen (2010): NGOs, foreign donors, and organizational processes: Passive NGO recipients or strategic actors? In: McGill Sociological Review, vol. 1, pp. 29-45.

Robinson, Fiona (2021): Feminist foreign policy as ethical foreign policy? A care of ethics perspective. In: Journal of International Political Theory, vol. 17, no. 1, pp. 20-37.

Sundstrom, Lisa McIntosh (2005): Foreign assistance, international norms, and NGO development: Lessons from the Russian campaign. In: International Organization, vol. 59, no. 2, pp. 419-449.

Tiessen, Rebecca (2019): What's new about the Feminist International Assistance Policy: The problem and possibilities of "More of the Same". In: University of Calgary School of Public Policy Publications, vol. 12, no. 44, pp. 1-15.

Tiessen, Rebecca; Lough, Benjamin J.; Cheung, Samuel (2018): Introduction: A theoretical and methodological case for examining agency and power relations in North-South volunteering research collaborations. In: Tiessen, Rebecca; Lough, Benjamin J.; Grantham, Kate (ed.): Insights on International Volunteering. Perspectives From the Global South. Germany, pp. 7-12.

Win, Everjoice J. (2004): Not very poor, powerless or pregnant: The African woman forgotten by development. In: Institute Development Studies Bulletin, vol. 35, no. 4, pp. 61-64.

Gender-focused Social Innovation and the Role of International Development Volunteers in Promoting Women's Economic Empowerment

Rebecca Tiessen, Tiffany Laursen, Benjamin J. Lough, with Tabitha Mirza

1. Introduction

Social innovation programming is an essential component of international development and economic empowerment projects and is linked to economic growth and improved job opportunities (Pandey/Kumar 2019). Integral to social innovation and economic expansion, women are increasingly targeted as an "untapped driver of growth" (Devex 2013; Collins 2016). However, despite a growing number of commitments to invest in women's economic empowerment, women are still often excluded from entrepreneurial investments, receive less funding for innovative business ventures, and are less likely to be engaged in full-time jobs compared to men (Lough/Wells, forthcoming; World Bank 2014; World Bank 2021). Furthermore, only 1 in 3 small, medium, and large businesses globally are owned by women, and this rate drops to 1 in 4 in lower-income countries (Halim 2020). Evidence of gender inequality in the economic sector can also be found in women's disproportionate time spent on unpaid care and household labor (2.5 times more than men), occupational segregation, lack of maternal leave provisions, and overall disparity in earnings between women and men (International Labour Organization 2017; Ferrant/Pesando/Nowacka 2014; United Nations 2015).

Addressing the economic insecurity of women and girls is central to several global strategies, including the Sustainable Development Goals (SDGs). These goals focus on providing equal value for unpaid care work and promoting shared domestic responsibilities, as well as ensuring full participation in leadership and decision-making by women. However, the economic empowerment of women also requires simultaneous commitments to addressing the social and systemic practices that perpetuate gender inequality by reducing inequitable access to economic resources and financial services while opening new economic activities and supports to scale up social innovation.

Gender-focused social innovation (GFSI) marks a departure from previous development strategies aimed at women's economic empowerment in several ways. First, GFSI moves away from essentialist notions of economic empowerment that assume women's incorporation in the market as business actors will eliminate gender inequality (Collins 2016). Second, bringing a transnational feminist lens, a GFSI approach to development programming rejects neoliberal discourses constructing subaltern women's work as that which falls outside the purview of traditional market activities that are considered to be 'productive' (Collins 2016). GFSI calls attention to the exploitation of gendered and unpaid labor upon which economies – local and global in scale – are dependent. Moreover, GFSI perspectives shift from narrow definitions of empowerment that instrumentalize gender in economic development projects and move toward a view of improved gender relations as a trigger, process, and product of social transformation. In this way, GFSI moves away from traditional market interventions and enhances our knowledge of innovations that are difficult to measure (Collins 2016; Blake/Hanson 2005).

As an example of GFSI in practice, process innovations may emerge from the interactions between marginalized and privileged groups who seek to combat cultural norms that perpetuate cycles of gendered economic exclusion (Pandey/Kumar 2019; Blake/Hanson 2005). In this way, GFSI acknowledges the gendered relations of power that underlie systemic inequalities and seeks to disrupt them by enhancing peoples' capacity to act. Consistent with this approach, this paper considers diverse strategies for the promotion of GFSI and women's economic empowerment across ten countries. We draw on examples of the programmatic commitments and the characteristics of program support, namely, the role of international development volunteers (IDVs) in advancing gender equality in economic empowerment and social innovation initiatives.

Several processes and outcomes, as well as challenges and opportunities for social innovation, emerge as they relate to the capacity building efforts of IDVs in relation to GFSI. An important starting point for evaluating GFSI and the contributions of transnational actors is to consider the aspirational nature of GFSI, its process orientation, and the significance of a GFSI approach to all stages of the development project, including decision-making, project planning, implementation, and monitoring and development of activities with diverse groups of project participants (Eriksson 2014; da Silva Filho/de Souza/de Souza Lessa 2018). Within GFSI initiatives, we underscore the role of IDVs in facilitating economic change beyond instrumentalist women's economic empowerment programs by considering strategies that disrupt social inequalities through these transnational interventions. The findings from this study document how IDVs facilitate women's economic empowerment as both a process and product of GFSI by challenging systemic social inequalities and sustainable development in partner communities.

2. Literature Review: Social Innovation and Gender Empowerment

Innovation is conceptualized as the development of new or improved products, services, and processes (Baregheh/Rowley/Sambrook 2009). Innovation in the economic sector facilitates financial growth and is a measure of economic and positive social change (Eriksson 2014). As a *social* response to complex and deepening economic, political, and environmental crises (Hillier/MacCallum/Moulaert 2013), social innovation (SI) is defined in relation to the fulfillment of "human development ambitions" (Neumeier 2012: 49). Characteristics of social innovation include participatory, collaborative, and capacity-building dimensions of change that support the needs and priorities of marginalized groups that offer novel solutions to social inequality (Hillier/MacCallum/Moulaert 2013). Social innovation is also characterized by commitments to local ownership, context specificity, and inclusion and ownership of the process by those who are meant to benefit from the interventions (da Silva Filho/de Souza/de Souza Lessa 2018; Cunha/Benneworth/Oliveira 2015; Hillier/MacCallum/Moulaert 2013; Correia/Gomez/Oliveira 2016).

Gender equitable processes drive innovation and contribute to innovative products (Eriksonn 2014). Strategies that aim to include women in social innovations can range from short-term or limited techniques such as targeting women and girls to facilitate their inclusion within existing systems, to longer-term and transformational approaches that change the methods of inequality to facilitate new opportunities for women's and girls' participation (Rao/Tiessen 2020; Alsos/Hytti/Ljunnggren 2013). However, not all of these strategies are wholly productive; several limitations of women's economic empowerment are captured by scholars who examine persistent inequalities within existing neoliberal economic processes (Hillier/MacCallum/Moulaert 2013; Morton/Muchiri/Swiss 2020). Moreover, a neoliberalist approach that sincerely links the achievement of "gender equality to economic growth" increases the risk of reproducing the "very structural issues that feminists, and gender and development, seek to trouble and transform" (Morton/Muchiri/Swiss 2020: 333).

An alternative to neoliberal forms of women's economic empowerment is outlined in GFSI, which considers angles, structures, and assumptions and how these are components of social transformation and elements of both process and outputs of innovation (Eriksson 2014; Hillier/MacCallum/Moulaert 2013; Correia/Gomez/Oliveira 2016). Through the GFSI lens, gender inclusion and improved social relations can transform inequitable processes that prevent marginalized groups from active participation in their own development and are focused on power and agency (Rao/Tiessen 2020; Hillier/MacCallum/Moulaert 2013). GFSI therefore recognizes and re-generates the "power marginalized people already possess" (Morton/Muchiri/Swiss 2020: 333). It does not overlook, or further neglect people based on "class, regional, sex, ethnic, and socio-economic differences" (Rao/Tiessen 2020: 355; Eriksson 2014). In this way, GFSI can be used as a tool to achieve intersectional and transformative development through changes to the decision-making processes, the implementation of plans, and the monitoring and development of activities for enhanced fairness and equity among diverse groups (Eriksson 2014; da Silva Filho/de Souza/de Souza Lessa 2018).

International strategies designed to promote GFSI, and women's economic empowerment often include a range of actors, including transnational actors, aid workers, and international volunteers. While recognizing the value contributed by the wide range of these transnational actors, the research in this study considers the role and impact of IDVs in the promotion of GFSI programming engaged in timely opportunities to rethink, develop, and standardize the core organizational processes through a gender-aware lens (Lough/Tiessen 2019; Eriksson 2014).

Social innovation programs that are predominantly focused on the promotion of gender equality and women's empowerment are an essential advancement in international development solutions. As such, they shine a spotlight on the specific gender inequalities and women-specific needs of development programming. As described by a collaboration of scholars of the gendered nature of social innovation: "Gendered social innovation encompasses the identification of unsolved societal challenges of gender inequality and unmet needs among women or men as underrepresented or disadvantaged groups in various areas, motivating the development of new solutions by inclusive innovation processes" (Lindberg/Forsberg/ Karlberg 2015: 472).

A feminist theoretical lens through which we can examine GFSI emphasizes the role that context (place and people) plays in producing the conditions that enable or negate gendered social innovations, the nature of the social innovations commonly adopted, the process of delivering programming, and the ongoing needs and opportunities for gender-sensitive social innovations. Embracing a feminist lens considers the social and economic environment and its role in valuing and promoting certain kinds of innovative activity as well as devaluing or discouraging other forms of innovation. Furthermore, the social identities of innovators affect, and are affected by, the social and economic environment, contributing to ways that innovations get defined and promoted. A gender-focussed lens in social innovation provides insights into social and geographic contexts, as well as the enabling or limiting characteristics of those contexts (Blake/Hanson 2005). Thus, feminist and gender-focused priorities in social innovation shape, and are simultaneously shaped by, the negotiations over the understanding of contextually specific feminist approaches. (Lindberg et al. 2015)

An analysis of gender relations filtered through the lens of feminist social innovation is also shaped by the kind of social innovations introduced, including the nature of the relationship taking place in transnational spaces, such as the role and contributions of transnational actors. Scholarship in GFSI has, therefore, reinforced some of the core elements or drivers of social innovation, namely being inclusive, exchanging ideas and values, expanding and changing relationships and roles played by program participants, and diverse forms of support from donors. Applying a gender lens to these drivers allows us to consider the following questions: how to be inclusive in line with gender inequalities (context and people); how to ensure that a diversity of voices are represented in the exchange of ideas; how to deepen our consideration of the gendered roles and gender relationships that exist; how these relationships can change to facilitate social innovation from diverse people and in various contexts; and how to provide diverse forms of transnational support that will enable a gender and feminist lens in social innovation programming. Answers to these questions can enable a transformational approach to transnational feminist scholarship on social innovation.

A transformational and transnational feminist approach to social innovation considers gender-specific dimensions in a comprehensive way, focusing not just on the needs and interests of women and girls but also on the societal and structural barriers to their social innovation opportunities and the pathways to achieving gender equality. In other words, a feminist approach allows us to understand the power dynamics that perpetuate inequality of opportunity or relational considerations that might promote more gender equality by breaking down the nature and impact of 'place and people'. The emphasis on the context of place (i.e., community and culture-specific analysis) and people (i.e., transnational actors in their relation to local community members) is central to the analysis in this paper.

In addition to paying attention to context, a feminist approach considers opportunities for an intersectional lens to analyze the overlapping factors that can contribute to failure, success, or barriers to achieving social innovations. These intersectional realities include a variety of factors in addition to gender such as race, age, (dis)ability, ethnicity, class, etc. (see Lough/Wells, forthcoming).

In sum, transnational feminism offers a useful theoretical lens for breaking down the role and impact of place and people in our analysis of gender-focused social innovations. We employ transnational feminism in this paper because it helps us understand the opportunities and barriers of GFSI, the nature of GFSI interventions and how they support or counter feminist values, and the role of transnational actors working in local spaces. Specifically, transnational feminism underscores the global and cross-national impacts of social, historical, political, and economic activities carried out by diverse actors navigating their relationships to achieve social goals. In this way, the study provides new insight into contextually-specific feminist interpretations and perspectives of social innovation programming.

3. Methods

Interviews were conducted in 2018 – 2019 with 150 partner organization staff in ten countries. Once all interviews were transcribed, data were coded to identify common themes throughout. Data were analyzed using discourse analysis. The introduction to this special edition has more detailed information on the methodology for data collection and the analysis of findings.

4. Findings

Findings from the data highlight the social innovation processes and results facilitated by IDVs working in community-based organizations. These findings provide insights into the nature and extent of IDVs' support to gender equality and women's empowerment (GEWE), and social innovation programming. IDVs were widely recognized for introducing new ideas in support of social innovation and building the capacity of local communities, including supporting organization staff with skills and competencies needed to advance social innovation programs and to support entrepreneurship training. The contributions made by IDVs were significant for social innovations in numerous development sectors, from agricultural programming to microfinance and tourism. However, despite many successes and opportunities created through the work of the IDVs, several challenges were also highlighted, particularly in relation to IDVs' understanding of cultural context and their local interpretations of how to achieve gender equality. Respondents that participated in the research believed that improved knowledge of local culture and enhanced skills among IDVs were needed to navigate different cultural contexts. They asserted that heightened cultural knowledge and competence were central needs in the delivery of future transnational support by IDVs working in international development programs.

In the sections that follow, we consider the nature and extent to which feminism is seen as a guiding lens for GFSI programs that have clear goals of women's economic empowerment across all ten countries. We outline how feminism is interpreted differently and situated within national and local realities and cultural practices. This is important for thinking about GFSI programs through a feminist lens because these findings reinforce the need to design GEWE programming within local contexts, keeping people and place at the forefront of development interventions.

4.1 New Insights for Innovative Programming in Place

Partner organization staff valued IDVs for their fresh perspectives, new ideas, and contributions to knowledge. As a participant from Tanzania noted: "What I value the most is [their] experience and perception of things". This participant went on to explain how the different backgrounds and perspectives allow for "fresh eyes on some old stuff," which enables organization staff to modify or improve programming. The new perspectives generated through interactions with IDVs are seen, however, in a generative way: "These experiences we are sharing from their country and our country, our perception of things, it develops both of us." This is an important insight as it shows the significance of shared and mutual learning in transnational spaces.

Among the shared knowledge and mutual contributions are new ideas in support of local innovations. Partner organization staff highlighted several examples of innovations shared by IDVs. These interventions were considered to have, as one participant from Tanzania explained, a "huge economic and social impact". This example highlighted the innovation shared by IDVs for biogas generation using waste to generate electricity. The community benefited from this project because it resulted in monetary savings. This intervention also facilitated training and knowledge building for all community members and established a protocol to ensure that young mothers are able to benefit from the training. Specifically, the project incorporated childcare support for mothers who wanted to access the training.

One example of a program in Ghana included creating a childcare facility and providing childcare services for mothers who wanted to participate in the trainings. This initiative was proposed by an IDV and was considered "quite unique" by local actors. This project ultimately led to a much more inclusive training program for a diverse set of community members. The inclusivity protocols included in this initiative were highly valued by partner organizations who saw impacts in terms of education, training, and knowledge sharing for those who were previously prevented from such opportunities. As one of the Ghanaian participants said: "I value most their contribution" to these new ideas and approaches – contributions that "are not measurable."

The second example of IDV support for innovative programming in Ghana included help with the design of a monitoring tool that could capture and measure gender inclusion in radio programming. A participant from Ghana added: "There was nothing like monitoring the gender responsiveness of a radio program. But with the help of the tools, we were able to give feedback to the radio team on how gender responsive their program was." The information generated from this evaluation tool allowed the radio program team to keep track of the number of women who called, the number of women interviewed, and the number of women who contributed to the program. The results of this initiative led to better equity in radio program representation with efforts to always have one man and one woman hosting a radio program together. Combined with this initiative was a training session that helped the staff members understand how gender inequality permeated organizational practice and helped the participants to "understand the way we are continuing the whole stereo-typing information dissemination that goes on focusing only on men."

Several programs implemented in Nepal tracked the impacts on women's participation in economic opportunities. Outcomes of these programs include socio-economic development, including the establishment of "114 sub-sector producers' groups (PGs) in vegetable farming (mainly cauliflower and tomatoes), milk production, and goat-raising in the three project districts" (CECI 2018). The programs focused on including women and marginalized groups (Dalits in particular) with a goal of maximizing benefits through project interventions. These efforts resulted in a high degree of participation among marginalized groups including a participation rate of 72% women, 65% youth, and representation of Dalits and single women (CECI 2018). The project focussed on skills development, management of agricultural practices, and livestock activities. Interview participants in Nepal highlighted a number of ways that IDVs contributed to these programs, including economic empowerment programs designed to reduce the financial dependence of women on men. Specific projects promoting economic empowerment could be found in commercial agricultural projects, women's leadership and ownership of projects, and the creation of opportunities for women to enhance skills in the economic sector, promoting women entrepreneurs and cooperative management.

The primary goal of the Nepal program was to create opportunities for women and youth to benefit from technical training to facilitate better inclusion of women in the economy, on economic decision-making bodies, and in political spaces. IDVs provide this support in partnership with the locally-based organization staff. All 15 of the interview participants in Nepal provided examples of the role that IDVs play in supporting gender-focus social innovation and entrepreneurship programming, including activities such as the development of a guiding manual for a cooperative, trainings, video production, and proposal writing, among other activities. In one example, the partner organization staff explained how the IDV wrote a project proposal that received funding to start up an essential oil business that benefited more than 75 women in the community through a new business venture. In addition to the proposal writing, the IDV also helped with the business development and marketing of the product.

Other IDVs in Nepal played a pivotal role in helping local organization staff translate their goals and priorities into actions. For example, IDVs were able to help the organization's staff develop a "concrete plan about how and where to begin" with gender equality programming and policies. The IDVs helped develop planning strategies (two-year action plans). Specific targets of these initiatives included increasing the number of women members in the cooperatives and including women in the policy and decision-making processes. As one participant for Nepal noted: "Only after the arrival of ... volunteers, we realized the need for and importance of GESI [gender equality and social inclusion] in the organization." This example reinforces the importance of transnational actors in providing knowledge and ideas for translating ideas into practice. The priority of a stronger focus on women's needs and gender equality was already established by the organization in Nepal, and the volunteer's role was to help translate that idea into a reality.

Participants from Nepal provided several additional examples of how the volunteers used their knowledge of gender equality and social inclusion to improve development programming. As one interviewee from Nepal explained, the volunteers conducted research on farmers who were involved in the milk production sector over a long period of time: their problems, quality production, and maintenance of those milk products, which further helped in developing the new proposals and launching the new programs. The IDVs actively engaged the local farmers in these communities and ensured they were involved in the milk production. Over, time the IDVs realized that the milk was not being consumed by other communities and the IDVs saw this as an opportunity to expand the business and gain access to local markets where the farmers could sell the milk. Cultural marginalization of these farmers had previously made it difficult for them to access markets. Other communities in the area saw the possibilities created for the milk farmers who would bring the milk to the market to sell and began bringing their own goods to the market, including meat from buffaloes and cows. The IDVs worked with those excluded communities to help them understand the steps needed to bring their goods to market and encouraged them to develop their businesses in new ways. The knowledge of one of the IDVs who grew up on a cattle farm in Canada was particularly welcomed. The IDV had advanced knowledge about cattle, their digestive systems, and how best to feed and care for the cows. In addition to this practical knowledge, IDVs played an advocacy role for women farmers who began conversations with communities and partner organizations about the nature and extent of women's involvement in the dairy sector. However, as the IDVs noted, only men have legal control over the agricultural business. Through these observations, partner organizations began to think of new training programs to support women's rights, empowerment, and legal changes to support women's ownership of businesses.

Similar examples were provided in Tanzania, where partner organization staff explained the valuable contributions of IDVs who were able to identify knowledge gaps or missed opportunities. The IDVs were able to share these observations with partner organizations, and together, new initiatives and training opportunities were created to bridge knowledge gaps. The projects in Tanzania focused heavily on fruits and vegetable markets and business growth, and ecotourism. To support the fruits and vegetable agricultural sector, programs were geared to increasing entrepreneurial opportunities, business, and agronomic skills among women and youth and to improving productivity and market information and linkages to markets for women and youth.

In Tanzania, partner organizations provided several examples of the role of IDVs in promoting economic empowerment and gender equality in the areas of fruit production and processing, ecotourism, and agricultural programming. One example included a poultry production opportunity that was introduced to Maasai women since women often do not reap the benefits of raising livestock. The opportunity to raise chickens gave women a new source of income and an economic opportunity that they could own and control. This project also included gender sensitivity training for men and women in the community to ensure that women's labour is linked to financial gains from these projects and also developing greater economic independence and decision-making power.

Examples from Tanzania also included a significant emphasis on the importance of gender equality training and knowledge sharing. In some cases, partner organization staff considered this understanding of gender equality as a core feature of a feminist approach to development. In other cases, some participants explained they were not familiar with the meaning of feminism or did not consider it a helpful guiding concept for the work they were doing.

In Malawi, IDVs were able to build organizational capacity by introducing new reporting templates that would allow the organization to capture data better. As a participant from Malawi explained, IDVs worked with office staff to develop a tool that tracks: "the contributions per member, per month, per group so that we are able to track...strides we are making. If we have a group, if the savings are not increasing, the group is dead." The small contributions made by IDVs were often explained in relation to their ability to integrate a helpful innovation – such as the tracking tool – into an organization's projects. They also remarked on the IDVs' ability to provide innovative suggestions to improve existing initiatives in new ways.

One partner organization in Vietnam explained the contribution of an IDV who integrated principles of corporate social responsibility (CSR) to the organization. The staff member explained how the IDV shared information about the need for the industry to "pay back to the communities." This knowledge helped the organizations in Vietnam think about fairness in corporations that extended well beyond gender equality to strengthen overall economic fairness.

Another IDV working in Vietnam filled important gaps in organizational assessments of fairness by identifying new priorities for the organizations and creating an opportunity to critically reflect on these priorities using a SWOT (strengths, weaknesses, opportunities, and threats) analysis. Through the SWOT analysis, organizations were able to consider a large number of variables needed for the equitable delivery of their programs and the actions needed to achieve their next steps. The recommendations that arose from this process allowed the organizations to consider their place in the broader organizational community, how they can be more competitive, and ways to communicate their ideas better. In just one year, the organization noted a large number of changes.

GFSI programs in Guatemala aimed to impact economic, social, and professional outcomes for more than 12,000 women and youth. These projects were designed to strengthen an inclusive market, increase economic competitiveness, and build the capacities of community members through technical support. Some projects focused on the agricultural sector designed to provide sustainable growth and to foster inclusive market systems. Other projects focused on enhancing the participation of women and youth in the agricultural industry through the creation of new opportunities in the coffee industry (production, management, administration, and commercialization). Similarly, the cardamom export sector has many opportunities for job creation for women and youth. Another project area included the food processing industry with a focus on job creation for women and youth, specifically in processing and packaging fruits and vegetables and in the preparation of marmalades and jellies. These projects resulted in increased incomes (by 25%) for agricultural producers, 40,000 trees planted, support to 1,332 coffee producers – 25% of whom were women – and collective outcomes that led to improved price negotiation skills, production infrastructures, technological innovation, processing, and improved governance and women's participation (CECI no date).

The support provided by IDVs in Guatemala led to entrepreneurial development, including the creation of 769 small and micro businesses and 1,539 jobs, with priority given to women and youth. Business plans were created by "907 micro-entrepreneurs and business service centers developed gender equity policies and implemented special projects for women and youth." (CECI no date). The IDVs were integral to the delivery of these programs, providing a range of resources and support through new ideas, networking, skills development, and capacity building. As one partner organization in Guatemala noted, the IDV "was here for one year, and she helped us on the commercial side of things. It was a pilot project I was doing ... it was the first time they gave us the opportunity to develop business opportunities for our members, and [the volunteer sending organization's] primary interest was to help smaller producers in the field."

The research conducted in Guatemala highlighted that the majority of IDVs engaged in GFSI programs focused on women's economic empowerment. IDVs provided support to: develop business opportunities and building partnerships with female-led businesses, enhance an organization's social programs that target both male and female youth, and conduct a human resources evaluation with a particular focus on gender relations within the organization's workplace. Specifically,

IDVs partnered with local organizations and community members to increase women's salaries by building a business development model with a local business that was widely celebrated in the community. Other IDVs offered workshops on how to start a business with a focus on the empowerment of women to take advantage of opportunities. IDVs also focused on finding new ways of managing and handling the finances of the project to ensure funds distributed were used for their intended purposes. Finally, IDVs generated business opportunities for community members in order to help smaller producers achieve economic empowerment. Overall, the Guatemala interview participants agreed (8/15 strongly agreed and 7/15 somewhat agreed) that the IDVs contributed to improving the partner organization's capacity to address gender equality.

Across these different interpretations and implementations of GEWE programming in place, the interview participants noted a high level of satisfaction with the work that IDVs do to promote gender equality. The contributions of IDVs to GEWE within specific contexts was found to be significant. Understanding the local cultural contexts were central features of partner organization's reflections on the role and impact of IDVs. Within these specific locations, interviewees indicated that IDVs help to build local capacity, address and break down barriers to promote GEWE and advocate for policy enhancements while engaging with local knowledge holders and compromising on approaches to fit within local contexts. The partner organizations attributed IDVs with bringing in fresh perspectives, curiosity and energy, commitment to empowerment, capacity building, skills development, and changes that resulted from new attitudes and behaviors to organizations and communities. As transnational actors working in place, IDVs play an important role in shaping new perspectives, attitudes, and reciprocal learning that are only available through the engagement of external actors. Participants also described indirect contributions to GEWE that transformed local attitudes towards gender norms and expectations through IDVs' lived examples and informal dialogue with community members. Further, IDVs were also able to provide support to local staff in the day-to-day running of business operations through communication and IT skills, allowing for the strengthening of the host partner organization's efforts towards GEWE.

4.2 IDV Considerations for Improved GFSI Outcomes

Though IDVs were highly praised for their effectiveness in promoting GFSI in partner countries, respondents also noted several challenges that limited IDVs' ability to fully impart sustainable change in their respective communities. Specifically, their level of expertise, limited time commitments, and language barriers were frequently identified as significant factors that impeded GFSI outcomes in social innovation programs. Respondents expressed their frustrations with volunteers' expertise and professional experience with GFSI, as many volunteers lacked formal training in gender equality work; however, it is important to note that while many IDVs lacked professional experience in gender equality, most were viewed as flexible and willing to learn to assist with GFSI initiatives.

Finally, respondents agreed that limited time commitments impacted the effectiveness of IDVs' integration into the community and, thus, their impacts on GEWE initiatives as well. They described a lack of continuity after volunteers leave because their organizations do not have enough personnel to fill the full-time positions required to sustain the projects that were started by volunteers. Some of the partner organization staff also highlighted the need for IDVs to spend more time learning about the local context and drawing fewer conclusions before they had sufficient knowledge. A participant from Peru noted: "to transform things; you need to understand and not judge." Similarly, in Senegal, a staff member said she expected more understanding from the IDVs and to see differences in how countries run their enterprises, since "from the logistic and operational points of view, it is not the same".

5. Discussion and Analysis

Partner organizations working to promote social innovation in GEWE in the Global South engage in a unique relationship and exchange focused on the differences in cultural gender norms within the Global North and South. This exchange is characterized by an embrace of gender equality perspectives that have emerged both locally and internationally. At times, these interactions resulted in clashes related to cultural norms creating tension, confusion, but oftentimes, innovative initiatives. Partner organizations often promoted (and implemented) core programming geared to improving gender relations and women's empowerment while also adapting what may be culturally irrelevant or unacceptable. Our findings reinforce the significance of context in relation to the interpretation of GFSI. This helps us understand and expand transnational feminist theory by advancing an intersectional approach and pursuing a broader strategy that more fully incorporates community-centered inclusive practices. A social-inclusion approach to GEWE (particularly evident in Nepal) offers an important insight into transnational feminism by highlighting the way that partner organizations navigate donor demands in partnership with IDVs as transnational actors working to advance GFSI programming.

The examples provided in the findings above highlight the specific contributions made by IDVs to promote GFSI and women's economic empowerment. The nature of the gender-focused innovations introduced by the IDVs opened up spaces for women's participation and addressed some of the systemic barriers to women's inclusion. Other examples included IDVs playing a role in providing resources or supports that could facilitate women's participation. In so doing, the projects moved from an approach of targeting women's participation in economic empowerment programs to eliminating some of the barriers to their participation by identifying the factors that prevent participation and finding ways (through social innovations) to circumvent or tackle those barriers.

Social innovations are important for enhancing women's participation and addressing the systemic barriers to participation. On the other hand, several important limitations were also noted as areas to be addressed to enhance the contributions of IDVs. The implications for improving empowerment programming emphasize how social innovations introduced by IDVs are best proposed through participatory and informed processes that involve IDVs asking critical questions and engaging partners in discussions about what is possible before making suggestions or imposing changes that may not be culturally appropriate or sensitive.

Taken together, findings from this study shine a light on the critical importance of people and place as a central lens for the implementation and analysis of GEWE programming where transnational volunteers work in people-to-people relationships with local actors. Policies that aim to advance gender equality cannot be regulated or administered in a vacuum. To work effectively, the gender equality policies that drive programming must consider the specific social, historical, political, economic, religious, and other conditions that define people's lived reality in particular contexts. While transnational actors often work to advance gender equality through standard methods such as recognizing the value of unpaid care work, promoting shared domestic responsibilities, ensuring women's full participation in leadership and decision-making, and empowering women economically, they must carefully "situate" these approaches within the milieu of place and human relationships. Furthermore, by situating interventions in context, IDVs can also deliver capacity building methods that enable partner organizations to "formulate and own" their own approach to internal partner organization transformation so that gender-focused innovation outcomes can answer the needs of the local context" long after the IDVs' mandate is over (Rao/Tiessen 2020: 365; Devereux 2008; Hillier/MacCallum/Moulaert 2013; da Silva Filho/de Souza/de Souza Lessa 2018; Lough/Tiessen 2020).

6. Conclusion

The findings examined here lend themselves to several key recommendations. The first recommendation is to ensure that IDVs have the necessary knowledge and training in gender equality and women's empowerment when tasked with working on GFSI projects. While technical training is an important first step, it must also be paired with contextual information and knowledge about local cultural norms and practices as well as culturally distinct approaches to addressing gender equality. International volunteer cooperation organizations (IVCOs), universities and colleges, faith-based organizations, and other institutions that send volunteers abroad need to structure their programs to enable IDVs to spend time listening and learning from partners about their own gender equality strategies and feminist practices. The pathways toward achieving gender equality differ across countries, and organizations and volunteers need to adjust strategies to each place. By tailoring their implementation strategies, volunteers can ensure that their interventions are culturally appropriate, while also helping to build social cohesion and gaining community buy-in.

IDVs play a valuable role in advancing gender equality programming, and they contribute to new perspectives in gender-focused social innovations. Likewise, community members and partner organization staff who are embedded in local places can contribute their own education, experience, knowledge, and training to enhance the capacities of international volunteers. To do feminist work effectively, IDVs and the organizations that facilitate their placements must promote the exchange of ideas, engage in reciprocal learning opportunities, work to understand and apply emic feminist frameworks that work effectively in place, and stay fully open to culturally-divergent pathways for achieving gender equality.

Social inclusion is not a magic bullet to promote GEWE but rather a strategy to further explore its potential boundaries, limitations, and promises. Ultimately, the findings in this study remind us that the implementation of feminist principles and GFSI hinges on the depth of understanding that transnational actors have about the cultural norms (context) and the spaces for integrating a gendered-focused approach that is culturally specific and valued. A transnational feminist approach to GFSI is linked to effective program implementation because GFSI programming requires a commitment to understanding local context and values, including a respect for the resilience and social transformation of local communities. Successful strategies focused on gender equality and social inclusion must begin with a context-specific feminist approach while also maintaining social cohesion, preventing conflict, and creating buy-in among staff and community members to cooperatively implement and sustain GFSI projects.

Bibliography

Alsos, Gry Agnete; Hytti, Ulla; Elisabet, Ljunggren (2013): Gender and innovation. State of the art and a research agenda. In: International Journal of Gender and Entrepreneurship, vol. 5, no. 3, pp. 236–256.

Baregheh, Anahita; Rowley, Jennifer; Sambrook, Sally (2009): Towards a multidisciplinary definition of innovation. In: Management Decision, vol. 47, no. 8, pp. 1323-1339.

Blake, Megan K; Hanson, Susan (2005): Rethinking innovation. Context and gender. In: Environment and Planning A, vol. 37, pp. 681–701.

CECI (2018): Annual Report 2017-2018. https://www.ceci.ca/data/ceci-nepal-annual-report-2017-18.pdf (28.10.2021).

CECI (N.D.): Prosol. https://ceci.ca/en/projects/prosol (6.17.2021).

Collins, Andrea M. (2016): "Empowerment" as efficiency and participation. Gender in responsible agricultural investment principles. In: International Feminist Journal of Politics, vol. 18, no. 4. pp. 559–573.

Correia, Suzanne Érica Nobrega; Gomez, Carla Regina Pasa; Oliveira, Veronica Macario De (2016): Dimensions of social innovation and the roles of organizational actor: the proposition of a framework. In: RAM. Revista de Administração Mackenzie, vol. 17, no. 6, pp. 102–133.

da Silva Filho, José Carlos Lázaro; Ana Clara Aparecida Alves, de Souza, Bruno, de Souza Lessa (2018): Social innovation and the promotion of local economic development. In: Innovation & Management Review, vol. 16, no. 1, pp. 1–17.

Devereux, Peter (2008): International volunteering for development and sustainability. Outdated paternalism or a radical response to globalisation? In: Development in Practice, vol. 18, no. 3, pp. 357–370.

Devex (2013): Women entrepreneurs: An untapped driver of economic growth. https://www.devex.com/news/sponsored/women-entrepreneurs-an-untapped-driver-of-economic-growth-81458 (6.29.2021).

Eriksson, Anna Fogelberg (2014): A gender perspective as trigger and facilitator of innovation. In: International Journal of Gender and Entrepreneurship, vol. 6, no. 2, pp. 163–180.

Ferrant, Gaëlle; Pesando, Luca Maria; Nowacka, Keiko (2014): Unpaid care work: The missing link in the analysis of gender gaps in labour outcomes. https://www.oecd.org/dev/development-gender/Unpaid_care_work.pdf (6.29.2021).

Halim, Daniel (2020): Women Entrepreneurs Needed-Stat! https://blogs.worldbank.org/opendata/women-entrepreneurs-needed-stat (28.10.2021).

Hillier, Jean; MacCallum, Diana; Moulaert, Frank (2013): Social innovation: Intuition, precept, concept, theory, and practice. In: ResearchGate, vol. 14, no. 41, pp.13–24.

International Labour Organization (2017): World Employment Social Outlook: Trends for Women 2017. http://www.ilo.org/wcmsp5/groups/public/---dgreports/---inst/documents/publication/wcms_557245.pdf (6.29.2021).

Lindberg, Malin; Forsberg, Lena; Karlberg, Helena (2015): Gendered social innovation – a theoretical lens for analysing structural transformation in organizations and society. In: International Journal of Social Entrepreneurship and Innovation, vol. 3, no. 6, pp. 472-483.

Lough, Benjamin J.; Tiessen, Rebecca (2019): International volunteering capacity development. Volunteer partner organization experiences of mitigating factors for effective practice. In: Forum for Development Studies, vol. 46, no. 2, pp. 299–320.

Lough, Benjamin J.; S, Wells (forthcoming): Intersectional analysis of gender, race, and geography on the funds raised by social ventures.

Cunha, Jorge; Benneworth, Paul; Oliveira, Pedro (2015): Social entrepreneurship and social innovation. A conceptual distinction. In: Carmo Farinha; Luís M.; Ferreira J. J. M., Smith, H. L.,; Bagchi-Sen S (ed.): Handbook of research on global competitive advantage through innovation and entrepreneurship. Pennsylvania, pp. 616-639.

Morton, Sam E; Muchiri, Judyannet; Swiss, Liam (2020): Which feminism(s)? For whom? Intersectionality in Canada's Feminist International Assistance Policy. In: International Journal: Canada's Journal of Global Policy Analysis, vol. 75, no. 3, pp. 329–348.

Neumeier, Stefan (2012): Why do social innovations in rural development matter and should they be considered more seriously in rural development research? – Proposal for a stronger focus on social innovations in rural development research. In: Sociologia ruralis, vol. 52, no. 1, pp. 48-69.

Pandey, Umesh Chandra; Chhabi, Kumar (2019): SDG5 – Gender Equality and Empowerment of Women and Girls. Bingley.

Rao, Sheila; Tiessen, Rebecca (2020): Whose feminism(s)? Overseas partner organizations' perceptions of Canada's Feminist International Assistance Policy, In: International Journal: Canada's Journal of Global Policy Analysis, vol. 75, no. 3, pp. 349–366.

World Bank (2014): Gender at Work: A Companion to the World Development Report on Jobs. https://documents.worldbank.org/en/publication/documents-reports/documentdetail/884131468332686103/gender-at-work-a-companion-to-the-world-development-report-on-jobs (17.10.2021).

World Bank (2021): Labor force participation rate, female (% of female population ages 15) (modeled ILO estimate). https://data.worldbank.org/indicator/sl.tlf.cact.fe.zs (6.29.2021).

United Nations (2015): The World's Women 2015.https://unstats.un.org/unsd/gender/downloads/worldswomen2015_report.pdf (28.10.2021).

Resistance, Cooperation and Collaboration with International Development Volunteers: Considering Masculinities and Transnational Feminism

Somed Shahadu Bitamsimli

1. Introduction

Contemporary studies and scholarship on International Development Volunteers (IDVs) have effectively emphasised their invaluable contribution to promoting Gender Equality and Women Empowerment (GEWE) in partner organizations and communities in the Global South (Tiessen/Rao/Lough 2020; Tiessen/Lough/ Cheung 2018; Butcher/Einolf 2017; Seelig/Lough 2015). Research evidence continues to highlight the transformative potential and mutual benefits of the intercultural interaction between IDVs from the Global North and partner organizations in the South. Staff of partner organizations and beneficiary communities in the Global South consider male IDVs particularly to be key allies in promoting GEWE because they demonstrate alternative (soft) masculine behaviours in their everyday interactions with the local people in ways that have a potential to transform local norms. Whereas these interactions have been mapped as an opportunity to positively transform local gender norms and behaviours, some studies have deployed critical theory to characterize the interaction as an exercise of 'colonial continuity' (Heron 2007) made possible only by the unequal distribution of power.

This paper examines the experiences of partner organization staff as they navigate transnational relationships with IDVs and the delivery of GEWE programming. Findings from this study also highlight experiences of resistance, cooperation and collaboration in the design of gender equality programming. At the heart of this analysis is a focus on agency as expressed through the perspectives of partner organizations who are active agents in navigating programming in collaboration with Global North transnational actors.

To fully explore agency and the experiences of partner organizations in transnational spaces, I apply a theoretical lens that captures the breadth of interactions, reactions and strategies employed. Previous studies have relied heavily on critical theory and neocolonial analyses to consider the transnational spaces where IDVs and partner organizations are operating and the structural limitations (Clost 2014; Simpson 2004; Cook 2007; Baaz 2005; Heron 2007). While these critical insights help understand important challenges and systemic inequalities in development programming, they offer limited insights into the range of experiences of partner organization staff as they negotiate gender equality priorities in line with local cultural norms and values and through transnational feminist lenses. This paper analyzes the tensions between agency and critical theory through a transnational feminist lens.

2. Literature Review

Critical theory is commonly used in scholarship on international volunteering as a lens to scrutinize North-South relationships with a particular focus on issues of power and privilege as they relate to the experiences of Global North transnational actors engaged in volunteer programs in the Global South. Scholars have used neocolonial interpretations of knowledge exchange to document problematic and inequitable structural processes that are facilitated by neoliberal globalization and that contribute to 'colonial continuities' (Heron 2007; Loiseau et al. 2016; Perold et al. 2013; Baaz 2005). Post-colonial theory has often been deployed in this sense to highlight how colonial and post-colonial imaginaries of development are reinforced in the process of international volunteering. Critical theory scholars have used colonialism and neo-imperialism as entry points to explain the underlying structural dynamics that produce and reproduce unequal international relations that largely serve the strategic interests of Northern governments and Global North citizens at the expense of the Southern 'others' (Clost 2014; Simpson 2004; Tiessen/Kumar 2013; Cook 2007; Baaz 2005; Heron 2007).

Although neocolonial analyses offer a valuable critical examination of structural limitations to equality through the colonial continuities of North-South relations, they fall short of exploring the agency and voices of partners in the Global South and are thereby "limited in their ability to decolonize the scholarship on international volunteers (Tiessen/Lough/Cheung 2018:11) and insufficient to explore the relational aspects of international development volunteering (Tiessen/Rao/Lough 2020; Palacios 2010; Devereux 2010; Howes 2008).

In comparison with neocolonial and critical analyses, a more comprehensive analytical lens that focuses on transnational spaces where IDVs and partner organization staff work together to negotiate and navigate structural realities and local priorities is necessary for understanding strategies employed or resisted as part of GEWE programming. The analytical lens of transnational feminism fills some of these gaps. Therefore, the analytical lens of transnational feminism is employed in this paper to consider the unique contributions of transnational actors such as IDVs in their interactions with Global South partners. A transnational feminist lens highlights the importance of understanding agency and the perspectives of partner organization staff, including their needs, preferences, perceived outcomes and the value attached to interpersonal dynamics (Tiessen/Lough/Cheung 2018; Butcher/Einolf 2017; Seelig/Lough 2015).

Transnational feminism stems from a renewed urgency to uphold the principles of gender equality, justice, and fairness building on feminist interpretations of gender equality. Transnational feminism combines alliance-building strategies across cultural differences with local level insights on cultural specificity as Global South scholars and activists turn their attention to dismantling patriarchy in their own nations and regions (Quataert 2014). Transnational feminism builds on the work of African feminists, specifically scholars who have challenged the systematic domination of women by men in some or all of society's spheres and institutions (Walby 1997; hooks 2004). African feminist theorising and activism have both influenced and brought to the fore critical debates on gender and intersectional politics (Oyĕwùmí 2003; Tamale 2011; Ratele 2013), and put women's agency at the centre of the discussion. As such, applying a transnational feminist lens advances knowledge of agency and structural inequality and how these relate to local feminisms, empowerment, and transnational relationships.

When assessing gendered transnational relations, little has been written about the influence of IDVs. IDVs, as transnational actors working in the Global South, offer avenues for new synergies in their relationships with partner organization staff to collectively unpack everyday issues that may be unchallenged such as power dynamics, gender relations, and root causes of inequality (Lough/Tiessen 2016; Schech et al. 2019; UNV 2015). The relationship between IDVs and partner organization staff in this process of making sense of gender inequality exposes tensions and mutual learning that arise from a partnership model of reflecting on power dynamics in GEWE programs. The design of GEWE programs between IDVs and partner organization staff is, however, fraught with tensions and resistance. Understanding the reason for resistance is important for considering the possibilities for – and limitations of – GEWE programming.

Through sustained relationships between IDVs and partner organization staff, the scope for mutual learning grows and thereby the opportunities for transnational feminist values to be asserted and enacted in these transnational spaces also grows. Transnational feminism offers new insights into alternative interpretations of feminism and gender equality, highlighting ways of being and knowing that place equal importance on subaltern voices and ensuring the discursive space to deconstruct and reconstruct local values. Transnational feminism fosters a better understanding of thematic and conceptual notions that underpin international development volunteering, and commitments to reciprocity, mutuality, and intercultural competencies, as well as ethics and social justice. Next, I examine the experiences of partner organization staff who navigate GEWE programming priorities introduced by IDVs: their reactions, resistance, and reflections on finding common ground when working in partnership with IDVs.

3. Methods

Interviews were conducted in 2018 – 2019 with 150 partner organization staff in ten countries. Once all interviews were transcribed, data were coded to identify common themes throughout. Data were analyzed using discourse analysis. The introduction to this special edition has more detailed information on the methodology for data collection and the analysis of findings.

4. Conservative Values and Resistance to Change

Data collected from the ten countries assessed in this study advances our understanding of how the transnational interactions and engagements between IDVs and staff of partner organisations help to dismantle and challenge negative cultural norms and gender stereotypes that undermine the success of GEWE initiatives. Two core findings across the sample help us understand the way that GEWE is understood and interpreted within local contexts: conservative values and resistance to change and respecting local culture and re-imagining GEWE in local contexts. The cross-cultural opportunities offered by international volunteering have often been leveraged by partner organizations to help improve the understanding of their staff and beneficiary communities about alternative norms and transformative cultural practices that can enhance gender equality. The two themes that emerged from this analysis will be discussed in turn. This paper first looks at conservative values and resistance to change, and then turns to a discussion of respecting local culture and re-imagining GEWE in local contexts.

GEWE programs introduced by or facilitated through the work of IDVs can provoke hostilities and resistance from a small, but often powerful, group of people within the partner countries. Conservative voices and patriarchal gatekeepers in the Global South often invoke culture and tradition as the pretext to reject GEWE programming. Those who resist GEWE initiatives may view these programs as externally imposed by Western powers. Such a view shows little understanding of the locally-based feminists (men, women, transgender, and non-binary) fighting for gender equality and women's rights in their own communities, including scholars, human rights defenders and civil society organizations (Kapur 2005; Mohanty 2003; Quataert 2014; Okech/Musindarwezo 2019).

Respondents in this study highlighted culturally grounded hegemonic masculine practices as one of the major challenges towards implementing GEWE initiatives. These problematic masculine behaviours and patriarchal hostilities are a constant distraction that reify a kind of resistance to GEWE, framed around a particular narrow and largely uninformed or uneducated claims of culture and traditions that wilfully ignores systemic inequality. For instance, a male senior administrator at one of the partner organizations in Kenya, elaborated on what he has observed from community members as forms of distrust for GEWE programming as a Western imposition, asserting cultural expectations of men's roles as leaders and heads of the family:

> *The challenges are we have what we call conservatives. Some of them are those conservatives who believe that the man is the head and women are not supposed to lead. They still live in the old schools of thought...*

These understandings of patriarchal norms are often linked to patriarchal structures resisting GEWE, and any kind of social change that would undermine male privilege thereby threatening these structures. As another staff member from Kenya noted:

> *African traditions are a patriarchal society where men are very dominant and anything that goes like women are trying to come to the same level through equality and all that then there is a lot of resistance in this community.*

Patriarchal expectations of the gender division of labour are further understood as a barrier to women's economic opportunities. For example, an interviewee in Vietnam noted:

> *At the family level, there are some barriers for women in businesses. Many men want women to stay home and spend more time with the family, taking care of children. They do not support women with business. That kind of challenge still exists in Vietnam.*

Understanding local hostility to GEWE is important to inform better education and awareness about women's rights and feminist principles. The resistance against GEWE can be viewed as the manifest reaction of patriarchy to the potential changes in gender relations, which is often felt as disruptive in people's lives as well as local beliefs and customs. Resistance to gender equality (GE) can generally be understood as active resistance and passive resistance. Respondents described active forms of resistance to involve openly challenging the goal or relevance of GEWE, putting forward alternative facts and arguments against it, and often trying to persuade others to join the opposition. Passive resistance on the other hand is often difficult to detect and can even go undetected depending on the resistor's proximity to power. It may take time to discover passive resistance against implementing GE programs because the people involved are often part of the GE project. They pretend to be supporters of gender equality, but in reality, their deeper feelings oppose the idea. Such saboteurs apply their subtle acts in their own work within the organizational set up, and quietly undermine or sabotage the implementation of gender policies or programs. Others may say they support gender equality but point out that there are more urgent and pressing priorities to be addressed first. One male project administrator in Ghana raised this point during the interviews:

The men are saying that any work that comes to the community is focusing on empowering women but then there are vulnerable men. Women in some of these communities are more empowered than some men in that community and for that matter we should begin to see beyond just gender.

As revealed by the data in this study, the major factors responsible for slowing the progress in achieving GEWE goals are: the misinformed nature of these perspectives, coupled with limited understanding of the essence for GEWE to be women-focussed to a large extent, and their lack of understanding of systemic inequality and how it disproportionately leads to discrimination against both men and women.

Staff working on GE projects have also highlighted the threat of deeply-held misogynistic, sexist and patriarchal behaviours that undermine the success of gender-specific development programs. One of these challenges is the persistence of hegemonic practices that legitimizes male superiority in all aspects of social relationships in the private and public sphere, the first of which are the social norms and practices that normalize male privilege, whereby families train boys to be future leaders and breadwinners, and girls to be future subordinated dependents of men. The consequence is lack of paid job opportunities to earn income, while men dominate both private and public sector work. Although many women have entered the workforce and may also be heads of households and breadwinners, the vision of domestic life, which continues to dominate the imagination of many cultures, is one in which the logic of male domination is intact, whether men are present in the home or not (hooks 2014). One male staff member of a partner organization raised this point in Kenya:

African traditions are a patriarchal society where men are very dominant and anything that goes like women are trying to come to the same level through equality and all that then there is a lot of resistance in this community.

Revolutionary feminist consciousness-raising emphasized the importance of learning about patriarchy as a system of domination, how it became institutionalized and how it is perpetuated and maintained. "Understanding the way male domination and sexism was expressed in everyday life would awaken women to the realities of their victimization and exploitation by the patriarchal structures" (hooks 2014:7). Women who defy the odds and make it into professional careers or seek to make their own income always risk the triple role burden imposed by the patriarchal gender order, whereby women must combine productive, reproductive, and community obligations along with other duties such as being a 'good housekeeper' (family welfare and harmony), which also add other layers of responsibility on the woman. This may be partly responsible for the lack of progress in breaking the glass ceiling for many women, as explained by one respondent from Nepal:

I think an employer will always seek a male employee instead of a female. He will look for male not female. They are very much thinking that the female will get married and go to the husband's house, much less time at the office and work.

In most of the other countries where data was collected for this study, similar concerns of discriminatory practices limiting women's access to resources and paid employment opportunities arose. For example, in Kenya, one participated noted:

When a woman is married, she has to go to her husband's home. It does not matter if she is a working woman or someone who does not work, she has to do all the home activities, she has all the responsibility. All the responsibilities at home and at work.

Sexist and discriminatory views translate into discriminatory practices. For example, men are more dominant in the business community and are more likely to serve on boards and decision-making bodies. This results in significant barriers to women's participation in new start-ups and, as one person in Vietnam noted, it is therefore "difficult for women to join the investing world. Some start-up women say that they had difficulty in accessing investors."

Adding an intersectional lens, it is clear that gender inequality can be more significant among certain ethic groups. As another organization partner from Vietnam notes:

For certain ethnic minorities, the men control all the business in the family. If someone comes to the house, he is expected to approach first. If you bring women outside the house, men need to be consulted.

Similarly, in Nepal, challenges arise in terms of gender inequality and ethnic minority groups as one organizational staff member added:

Working with ethnic minority female students is very challenging when they tend to get married so young. There exist social norms in the mountainous areas that they do not want girls to study further, they will create more opportunities for boys.

These patriarchal norms and cultural practices within many countries make tackling gender inequality a complex and challenging endeavour. The interview participants provided many examples of the specific challenges they encounter; the resistance they met from different members of the community (primarily men in positions of leadership, but also women who seek to uphold cultural values as a means to maintain social and family cohesion). Despite experiences of resistance to change, gender norms, and cultural practices are dynamic (Okech/Musindarwezo 2019; Ahmed/Meena 2012).

4.1 Respecting Local Cultures and Re-Imagining GEWE in Local Contexts

Several study participants noted that a lack of cultural understanding by some IDVs have negative ramifications on the impact they make, emphasizing that the lack of cultural knowledge is a serious limitation for IDVs in promoting GEWE. Others suggested the need to withdraw IDVs from the frontlines of promoting gender equality, and rather restrict their role to training local staff of partner organizations who, in their view, would be better positioned to navigate the potential conflict or tensions associated with promoting GE in a patriarchal society.

One of the core findings across the ten countries was the emphasis on creating buy-in among men of GEWE programming. As previous scholars have argued, dismantling and changing patriarchal gender order will require both men and women to work together (hooks 2004). Without men and boys as allies in the struggle, the feminist movement will not progress because it would be a missed opportunity to work together to correct the assumptions deeply embedded in the cultural psyche that feminism is anti-male. IDVs are seen as playing a vital role in promoting increased involvement of men in GEWE programs. One example that was mentioned by several study participants was the significance of having men IDVs engaged in GEWE work as a way to promote alternative masculinities and break down gender barriers, especially when it comes to the gender division of labour.

While hegemonic masculine norms may oppress local men, who would otherwise wish to express equality in their relationships by performing roles normally assigned to women, male IDVs remain one of the key conduits through which alternative masculine ideas can be demonstrated or practiced. Whereas it is no longer a strange phenomenon in Western societies for a man to participate in basic household chores (e.g. cooking, washing dishes or cleaning the house), local men in patriarchal societies often risk consequences if they transgress these socially constructed gender barriers. Most GEWE projects consider IDVs to be allies and role models because they demonstrate alternative masculinities that can transform gender relations within the workspace and in beneficiary communities. The following are some of the ways participants perceived to be positive promotion of alternative masculine norms. For example, a study participant in Kenya explained: "One example is that they even helped to change babies' diapers. He actually helped to do that. It looked like ooh no this is a woman's job, but he did it."

In Kenya, some partners also perceive IDVs to have influenced their community to change perceptions about gender norms. This is usually the case when male volunteers often take up traditionally female roles such as doing household chores. The host organizations and communities in the South draw inspiration from the exemplary gender-sensitive behaviour of IDVs, a situation that enhances the possibility of equal division of labour between men and women.

We learned some things from them [IDVs]. In Africa [and] Kenya gender roles are so divided, and it is almost like a taboo for men to do some things like even carry a child. We learned that what a man can do, or a woman can do; we can collaborate and just do everything together.

Similarly, in Ghana, one participant shared: "There are certain things we say is a woman's thing but from the volunteer's behaviour for example, he washes his own plate after he's done. The people are surprised that he would do his own stuff."

Some feminist organizations and GEWE advocates consider IDVs as allies because their presence in workspaces and communities provide an alternative approach that positively transform gender norms and problematic masculine behaviours. In Ghana, participants explained that "When you are a woman in our community, and you are talking about gender equality you look very strange to your male counterparts. But somebody from another culture brings that [and] it helps." Likewise in Kenya, partner organization staff consider outsiders' perspectives helpful for explaining why violence against women is a violation of human rights. In Tanzania, partner organization staff used examples of the country's commitments to United Nations resolutions and national policy documents as further evidence that practices such as violence against women were not acceptable in the country.

The day-to-day actions of IDVs were often perceived as fresh perspectives on alternative roles carried out by men and women. Through these observations, IDVs were able to break down barriers and rethink what is normal practice. While important opportunities for alternatively role modelling on gender roles was highlighted by several staff members across a number of countries, other ongoing challenges for addressing GEWE were explained in terms of perceptions of leaving men and boys behind. Concerns about perceived special treatment for women highlighted resentment and hostilities towards GEWE initiatives. These concerns ranged from specific complaints about the lack of attention to male poverty and vulnerability to fears that GEWE is a zero-sum game calculated to disempower men. In Ghana, one participant described the concerns as a form of backlash:

The men are saying that any work that comes to the community is focusing on empowering women but then there are vulnerable men also and that IDVs are too focused on women and leave out men.

Some respondents in Kenya echoed these concerns of GEWE programming – being too focused on women and girls, while livelihood opportunities are increasingly becoming scarce for many boys and men who are equally vulnerable. A male GEWE program officer from Uganda emphasised the need for GEWE programmes to advocate for mutual understanding and cooperation between men and women instead of focussing on women and girls' empowerment. In his view, GEWE programs run the risk of creating "a generation where women are more empowered than men... then we would need to go back to fighting for the rights of men."

Another respondent from Malawi echoed this view: "If it keeps pushing men away from taking on leadership roles then I feel like in the future is going to become another problem. So having a balanced set up is more ideal."

5. Analysis

Two main points can be deduced from these voices: the first is the significance of increasing the participation of men and boys as a means of promoting local acceptance and consensus on gender equality programs. The second, however, is an erroneous perception that women's empowerment automatically results in men's disempowerment. As noted earlier in the introduction, such problematic perceptions of feminism and GE serve as acts of resistance to the meaningful changes that are needed. Power in this context is seen as a zero-sum game whereby power won by some results in power taken from others. Education to promote a better understanding of empowerment as a universal goal is important, and that needs to start with the messaging.

Others see engaging men and boys as a critical factor to the success of GEWE, recognizing that men are part of the problem. In this view, boys and men can be useful allies in finding a solution. The participation of men and boys in support of gender equality has the potential to bring positive changes in their attitudes, perceptions and behaviours that benefit women and girls (Lang 2003; Flood 2007; Silberschmidt 2011). Engaging men and boys is also important because understanding men's gender expectations – their expected roles, relations and positions as men – can help engage them more naturally in efforts to curb masculine-related violence, achieve equality and reduce poverty (Lang 2003). IDVs also play a crucial role in supporting gender equality programming that promotes men's participation in gender equality.

It is also important to highlight the sentiments of mutual complementarity expressed in the subaltern perspectives presented in these findings; they reinforce the fact that volunteer projects that are designed to accomplish a common social goal like gender equality, and involve multiple ethnic groups, have the potential to break down barriers that separate diverse ethnic and social groups. Partner organizations, beneficiary communities, and local feminist groups regard IDVs as critical allies in the struggle against patriarchal resistance towards GE, which often manifests in the form of toxic or problematic masculine behaviour. IDVs' cross-cultural knowledge and understanding, as well as their inclination to bring social justice perspectives when discussing issues of GE, make them crucial enablers of otherwise nonexistent safe spaces to deconstruct local gender norms in ways that can lead to change in mindsets and attitudes towards GEWE. IDVs bring diverse perspectives that contribute to increased tolerance and broadened perspectives on how to solve problems, especially involving gender relations. They help to develop human resources of partner organizations by contributing skills, information, and knowledge to support organizational capacity building. IDVs help to increase the ability of partner organizations to successfully design programs and deliver GEWE programs. Volunteering for development, especially in the area of gender equality and women's empowerment, has contributed significantly to improving women's skills, understanding of their rights, and decision-making power.

Although challenges remain in how the cross-cultural interaction between the North and the South is structured, the Southern voices presented in this project provide a counterpoint to post-colonial and neoliberal critiques (Cook 2007; Baaz 2005; Haas/Georgeou 2019; Georgeou/Engel 2011; Lyons et al. 2012; Simpson 2004; Heron 2007). Post-colonial and neoliberal critique may inaccurately characterize subaltern actors as powerless and passive recipients of Northern aid tied to a Western conception of being (Tiessen 2018; Lough 2011; Lough 2013; Lough 2019). The direct contact among people from different backgrounds has the potential to make people more comfortable with each other's differences, to reduce anxiety, and to lead to mutual understanding and respect (Tajfel/Turner 1979).

Further investigation is required to fully uncover the specific ways in which IDVs and partner organizations navigate their cultural differences to promote GEWE. However, the partnerships forged through IDV creates transnational spaces across the local–international divide that are crucial to achieving international targets and realizing commitments to gender equality. To effectively harness the potential in these partnerships, researchers and development workers must recognize and acknowledge both the potential dominant Westernized perception and imposition of GE, as well as the potential for new knowledge production and contributions to solidarity movements. Transnational feminism is the most suitable lens through which one can make sense of the impact IDVs make in promoting GE. The application of this lens examines the relationship between a politics of location and accountability, and the politics of knowledge production by examining the histories and hierarchies of power and agency. Some feminist scholars have also defined the transnational in relation to women's cross-border organizing (Mindry 2001; Mohanty 2003), and as a spatialized analytic frame that can account for varying scales of representation, ideology, economics, and politics, while maintaining a commitment to difference and asymmetrical power (Radcliffe et al. 2003).

Deconstructing and transforming gender relations is likely to be limited in scope and impact unless gender equality programs adequately recognize, and engage with, the complexities and situational realities of men and masculinities in diverse spaces. Evidence continues to highlight different ways in which men's entanglement with dominant masculinities make men profoundly vulnerable and expose women to negative acts and behaviours (Clowes 2013; Ratele 2013). The southern voices in this research and in previous studies have emphasized that excluding men, boys, and notions of masculinities from feminist work risk producing limited and unsustainable outcomes (Morrell/Jewkes/Lindegger 2012; Greig/Edstrom 2012; Ratele 2014). A transnational feminist lens offers an alternative approach to examining patriarchy and masculinities in cross-cultural contexts. It reaffirms the importance of engaging men and boys in feminist practices and GEWE programming, while also exposing the dangers and consequences of patriarchy to individual men and women (hooks 2004).

6. Conclusion

The findings outlined in this paper document the important role IDVs can play in building crucial relationships that enhance the capacity of locally based staff to undertake GEWE projects. The relationships that IDVs forge with partner organization staff can also generate new opportunities to interrogate local norms and to unpack cultural practices that undermine GEWE. These observations also echo the findings by Rao/Tiessen/Lough (2020) that IDVs have helped staff members of partner organizations to gain increased confidence to openly discuss gender-related matters such as gender-based violence, family planning, and sexual behaviors. Without the cultural disruption caused by volunteers, many of these issues are otherwise considered to be either sensitive or an abomination to talk about in the local culture.

Despite the power inequality and cultural conflict highlighted in critical scholarship about international volunteering, this paper finds the cross-cultural contact between IDVs and partner organizations to represent a significant value and long-term support for the host organizations. These exchanges are not merely in the form of unidirectional aid from IDV; they thrive on reciprocal relations of mutual learning. The reciprocity and mutuality in these interactions narrow the cultural gap and strengthen North-South relations. This observation is consistent with contemporary scholarship on the impact of international volunteering (Lough et. al. 2011; Graham, et. al 2012; Burns/Howard 2015; UNV 2015; Butcher/Einolf 2017; Tiessen/Rao/Lough 2020). When understood as a relational and collaborative endeavour this draws our attention to the potential of international volunteering. These transnational collaborations are critical to turn international targets and commitments to GE into practical action (Rao/Tiessen 2020). Transnational feminism negates the inherent contradictions and limitations in feminist processes where 'difference' is based on external standards and is therefore viewed as an external frame of reference (Okech/Musindarwezo 2019).

IDVs are therefore seen as important allies whose presence in partner countries helps to create intercultural exchanges and interactions that have the potential to transform gender norms and to model alternative masculine behaviours that support the values projected by GEWE initiatives. IDVs are therefore crucial transnational change agents who contribute to GEWE outcomes. This empirical research fills an important gap in the literature in the examination of norm changes from both sides of the volunteerism relationship (Schech et al. 2019; Tiessen/Rao/Lough 2020). Improved knowledge outlining how attitudes and behaviours change can help uncover the spaces where transformations in gender relations happen and can open new opportunities to build long-term and sustainable gender equality programming, while also broadening our knowledge on the ways in which volunteers and staff from overseas interact, engage, and dialogue in everyday settings (Loiseau et al. 2016; Tiessen/Rao/Lough 2020).

The interaction and exchange between international volunteers and local communities have been linked to increased confidence among partner staff members when it comes to gender-related issues, especially when speaking about sensitive topics like gender-based violence, sexual behaviors, or family planning (Rao/Tiessen 2020). In the words of one respondent in Ghana, IDVs bring a distinct value system which encourages transformative thinking and inclusive approaches that improve gender relations and social cohesion. They bring different views and perspectives that enable local development organizations to provide opportunities that can create change in attitudes and behaviours towards gender equality.

Bibliography

Ahmed, Aziza; Meena, Seshu (2012): We have the right not to be 'rescued': When anti trafficking programmes underline the health and well-being of sex workers. In: Anti-Trafficking Review, vol. 1, no. 103, pp. 149-168.

Baaz, Maria Erikson (2005): The Paternalism of Partnership. A Postcolonial Reading of Identity in Development Aid. New York.

Burns, Danny; Howard, Jo (2015): Introduction. What is the Unique Contribution of Volunteering to International Development? In: IDS Bulletin, vol. 46, no. 5, pp. 1-4.

Butcher, Jacqueline; Einolf, Christoph (2017): Perspectives on volunteering. Voices from the South. New York.

Clost, Ellyn (2014): Visual Representation and Canadian Government-Funded Volunteer Abroad Programs: Picturing the Canadian Global Citizen. In: Tiessen, Rebecca; Robert Huish (ed.): Globetrotting or Global Citizenship: Perils and Potentials of International Experiential Learning. Toronto, pp. 230-258.

Clowes, Lindsay; Ratele, Kopano; Shefer, Tamara (2013): Who Needs a Father? South African Men Reflect on Being Fathered. In: Journal of Gender Studies, vol. 22, no. 3, pp. 255-267.

Cook, Nancy (2007): Gender, Identity and Imperialism. Women Development Workers in Pakistan. New York.

Devereux, Peter (2010): International volunteers. cheap help or transformational solidarity toward sustainable development. Murdoch University.

Flood, Michael (2007): International encyclopedia of men and masculinities. London.

Georgeou, Nichole; Engel, Susan (2011): The impact of neoliberalism and new managerialism on development volunteering. An Australian case study. In: Australian Journal of Political Science, vol. 45, no. 2, pp. 297-311.

Georgeou, Nichole; Haas, Benjamin (2019): Power, Exchange and Solidarity. Case Studies in Youth Volunteering for Development. In: Voluntas, vol. 30, no. 6, pp. 1406-1419.

hooks, bell (2004): The will to change. men, masculinity, and love. New York.

Howes, Andrew (2008): Learning in the contact zone. Revisiting neglected aspects of development through an analysis of volunteer placements in Indonesia. In: Compare, vol. 38, no. 1, pp. 23-38.

Heron, Barbra (2007): Desire for development. Whiteness, gender and the helping imperative. Waterloo.

Kapur, Ratna (2005): Erotic Justice. Law and the New Politics of Postcolonialism. London.

Lang, James (2003): Evolving the gender agenda – men, gender and development organisations. http://www.un.org/womenwatch/daw/egm/men-boys2003/EP10-Lang.pdf (14.05.2021).

Loiseau, Bethina; Sibbald, Rebekah; Abdul Raman, Salem; Darren, Benedict; Loh, Lawrence; Dimaras, Helen (2016): Perceptions of the role of short-term volunteerism in international development. Views from volunteers, local hosts, and community members. In: Journal of Tropical Medicine, pp. 1-12, doi:10.1155/2016/2569732.

Lough, Benjamin James; Tiessen, Rebecca (2016): Theoretical alternatives to deconstructive analysis of volunteering for development. Paper presented at the 12th international conference of the International Society for Third Sector Research. Stockholm.

Lough, Benjamin James (2011): International volunteerism in the United States, 2008. In: Center for Social Development, vol. 10, no. 11, pp. 1-8. www.scribd.com/doc/33744391/International-Volunteering-from-the-United-States (14.05.2021).

Lough, Benjamin James (2013b): Measuring and Conveying the Added Value of International Volunteering. Strasbourg.

Lyons, Kevin; Hanley, Joanne; Wearing, Stephen; Neil, John (2012): Gap year volunteer tourism. Myths of global citizenship?. In: Annals of Tourism Research, vol. 39, no. 1, pp. 361-37.

Mindry, Deborah (2001): Nongovernmental Organizations, 'Grassroots,' and the Politics of Virtue. In: Signs, vol. 26, no. 4, pp. 1187-1211.

Mohanty, Chandra (2003): Feminism without Borders. Decolonizing Theory, Practicing Solidarity. Durham.

Okech, Awino; Musindarwezo, Dinah (2019): Transnational feminism and the post-2015 development agenda. In: Soundings, vol. 71, no. 71, pp. 75-90.

Oyěwùmí, Oyeronke (2003): African Women and Feminism Reflecting on the Politics of Sisterhood. New York.

Palacios, Carlos (2010): Volunteer tourism, development and education in a postcolonial world. conceiving global connections beyond aid. In: Journal of sustainable tourism, vol. 18, no. 7, pp. 861-878.

Perold, Helene; Graham, Lauren; Mavungu, Eddy Mazambo; Cronin, Karena; Muchemwa, Learnmore; Lough, Benjamin J. (2013): The colonial legacy of international voluntary service. In: Community Development Journal, vol. 48, no. 2, pp. 179-196.

Quataert, Jean (2014): A knowledge revolution. Transnational feminist contributions to international development agendas and policies, 1965-1995. In: Global Social Policy vol. 14, no. 2, pp. 209-227.

Rao, Sheila; Tiessen, Rebecca (2020): Whose feminism(s)? Overseas partner organizations' perceptions of Canada's Feminist International Assistance Policy. In: International journal, vol. 75, no. 3, pp. 349-366, https://doi.org/10.1177/0020702020960120.

Ratele, Kopano (2014): Currents against Gender Transformation of South African Men. relocating Marginality to the Centre of Research and Theory of Masculinities. In: NORMA, vol. 9, no. 1, pp. 30-44, https://doi:10.1080/18902138.2014.892285.

Ratele, Kopano (2013): Masculinities without tradition. In: Politikon, vol. 40, no. 1, pp. 133-156.

Schech, Susanne; Skelton, Tracey; Mundkur, Anuradha; Kothari, Uma (2019): International volunteerism and capacity development in nonprofit organizations of the global south. In: Nonprofit and Voluntary Sector Quarterly, vol. 49, no. 2, pp. 252-271, https://doi.org/10.1177/0899764019867774.

Seelig, Vera; Lough, Benjamin J. (2015): Strategic directions for global research on volunteering for peace and sustainable development. In: Workshop report, CSDWorkshop Report, no. 15-45, pp. 1-13, https://doi.org/10.7936/K7JQ10J0.

Silberschmidt, Margrethe (2011): What would make men interested in gender equality. In: Cornwall, Andrea; Edström, Jerker; Greig, Alan (ed.): Men and Development – Politicizing Masculinities. London, pp. 98-110.

Simpson, Kate (2004): Doing development. The gap year, volunteer-tourists and a popular practice of development. In: Journal of International Development, vol. 16, no. 5, pp. 681-692.

Tamale, Sylvia (2011): African Sexualities. A Reader. Nairobi.

Tajfel, Henri; Turner, John (1979): An integrative theory of intergroup conflict. In: W. G. Austin; S. Worchel (ed.): The social psychology of intergroup relations. Monterey, pp. 94-109.

Tiessen, Rebecca; Kumar, Paritosh (2013): Ethical Challenges Encountered on Learning/Volunteer Abroad Programs for Students in International Development Studies in Canada: Youth Perspectives and Educator Insights. In: Canadian Journal of Developing Studies, vol. 43, no. 3, pp. 416-430.

Tiessen, Rebecca; Lough, Benjamin J.; (2018): Introduction. A theoretical and methodological case for examining agency and power relations in North-South volunteering research collaborations. In: Tiessen, Rebecca; Lough, Benjamin J; Grantham, Kate (ed.): Insights on International Volunteering. Perspectives From The Global South. Germany, pp. 7-22. https://dx.doi.org/10.5771/9783845283920-7.

Tiessen, Rebecca (2018): Learning and volunteering for development. Unpacking host organization and volunteer rationales. London.

UNV (2015): Volunteering to advance gender equality. New perspectives for the post-2015 agenda. https://www.unv.org/news/volunteering-advance-gender-equality-new-perspectives-post-2015-agenda (28.10.2021).

Walby, Sylvia (1997): Gender transformations. London.

Power in All Its Forms: Women's Political Participation, Activism, and Advocacy to Promote Gender Equality Facilitated by International Development Volunteers

Rika Mpogazi

1. Introduction

International development is a broad undertaking that encompasses a series of processes that require cooperation between individuals from many communities. Most importantly, it helps build linkages between local and international organizations in their pursuit of common development goals. In recent decades, one of the most important strides towards positive global development has been through the promotion of Gender Equality and Women Empowerment (GEWE). Eliminating gender biases and barriers to the development of women in order to enable them to achieve their full potential has therefore become a central principle of many development initiatives.

In this paper, the elements that are conducive to the successful achievement of GEWE will be presented through the evaluation of international development volunteers' (IDVs) contributions to women's political engagement, activism, and advocacy. Veritable political participation is not limited to the domain of state-led high politics; it can also manifest through active collaboration with informal networks and non-governmental organizations (NGO) or collectives. The analysis provided in this paper seeks to highlight the ways in which IDVs provide additional support to the local initiatives' efforts to enable women to yield power within their communities, whichever way they choose to define said 'power'. It identifies the various ways in which women utilize the often-limited tools at their disposal to create unique models of leadership that are representative of their specific needs and that of their communities.

2. Literature Review

Foucault's notion of true power as it pertains to empowerment implies "the exercise rather than possession of power", meaning that it can take many implicit forms (Parpart/Rai/Staudt 2002). This is of particular importance when analyzing political leadership as the act of molding society can also be done using the realm of society and culture through immaterial or abstract means. Empowerment therefore indicates an empowerment of self through "individual conscientization" and the empowerment of others through the mobilization of a collective and their resources (Parpart/Rai/Staudt 2002: 5). When looking at local scenarios we must also consider the interrelation that exists between local and global economic, political, and cultural forces.

The scope of women's political engagement is subjective to the form of political structure of each country. In Senegal, for example, as is the case in many other countries in Africa, a decentralized form of governance can often complicate the process of political participation. It is also said to perpetuate the legacy of colonialism through a continuation of the hierarchical and non-accountable political "patronage" that enabled designated local representatives to be in service of, and only answerable to the central power, the state (Patterson 2002). More specifically to women, the decentralization of power shuffles the players around the political board but keeps the gender inequality firmly intact as women often lack opportunities to penetrate the patriarchal patronage circle. Even the minority of women who manage to acquire a seat at the table are often expected to serve the interests of their male party leaders in order to maintain their seat. The few who remain firm in their accountability towards the needs and interests of women often lack resources and support to do so (Patterson 2002).

In addition, women's leadership and engagement are not restricted to party politics. In fact, many urban women yield power through their involvement in "educational institutions and the workplace" (Patterson 2002: 493). Others, mainly rural women, have sought to provide resources for their communities through the creation of grassroot credit funds and mutual aid, rather than depending on government assistance. Similarly, in Tanzania and Uganda, women's urban associations became a vehicle for solidarity in the pursuit of gender equality and inclusivity, since women have historically been excluded from formal political structures. Their associational life was born out of necessity due to the increasing double burden taken on by women who found themselves occupying the roles of reproductive and productive work during times of economic crisis or civil unrest (Tripp 1994). The output resulting from this social mobilization includes the creation of "income-generating activities, savings and the provision of social services such as daycare" (Tripp 1994: 108). This form of social and political assistance can be described as 'informal volunteering' as it is not coordinated by a larger-scale network of governmental or non-governmental organizations but that delivers support to their community nonetheless (UN Volunteers 2018: 101).

Civil society and voluntary engagement represent less-insulated, more on-the-ground alternatives to public service that are often embodied by local NGOs, thus encouraging a partnership between international development agencies and domestic civil society in the common pursuit of development objectives (Kamruzzaman 2018). In many cases, NGOs are an essential component of this process. As Kamruzzaman (2018: 72) asserted, "the NGOs' activities can be seen in all sectors of the country, society is benefiting from NGOs, and NGOs are benefiting from the social support". This is one of the motivating factors behind the incorporation of local NGOs to international non-governmental organizations (INGOs) as their local presence and practical knowledge help effectively and appropriately adapt global discourses to local contexts (Kamruzzaman 2018).

A study on political advocacy activity in the non-profit sector identified that successful strategies used to influence public policy include "lobbying in the Parliament; activity vis-à-vis government agencies, local authorities, and the media; initiating legislation; research and dissemination of information; and protest" (Schmid et al. 2008: 595). This study also revealed that development practitioners who worked in women's organizations had the most significant impact in all areas related to empowerment through media advocacy (Schmid et al. 2008). The study further indicated positive correlation between the number of international volunteers engaging with these organizations, and the output of political activity and policy prescriptions presented to local governments (Schmid et al. 2008). However, an IDV's ability to succeed in delivering appropriate support to the community or group they are servicing is dependant on their degree of critical reflexivity.

Critical reflexivity refers to the "complex relationship between processes of knowledge production, contexts of such processes, and involvement of producers" (Collier/Muneri 2016: 640). In other words, one must reflect on their positionality in relation to the cultural and social context in which they find themselves and their willingness to include the perspectives of local actors in their capacity building activities. The application of this framework allows for a de-colonization of the spaces in which Western and non-Western actors interact by allowing for a horizontal relation of knowledge sharing. The following section presents the research methods and findings that demonstrate the importance of critical reflexivity in relation to the analysis of GEWE in an international context.

3. Methods

Interviews were conducted in 2018 – 2019 with 150 partner organization staff in ten countries. Once all interviews were transcribed, data were coded to identify common themes throughout. Data were analyzed using discourse analysis. The introduction to this special edition has more detailed information on the methodology for data collection and the analysis of findings.

4. Findings

In this section, I consider findings across the transcribed data from ten countries as it pertains to political empowerment of women. Major themes emerge from this analysis of the data: the role of transnational actors (IDVs) in providing diverse mentorship and social support roles that promoted women's political engagement;

the role of transnational actors in the conscientization, critical reflexivity, and mobilization of civil society on gender related issues through research assistance; and critical insights into transnational feminist approaches that reflect an adaptive (and localized) strategy to encourage local women's political agency.

I will highlight the ways in which IDVs help support local partners by bringing awareness to the cause for which they are advocating and by providing empirical evidence to enhance the call for GEWE. I will also touch upon themes of privilege, power and positionality, as well as the notion of the glocalization of gender equality, meaning the formulation of NGO networks between local and international entities in order to recognize, value, and enhance the support to local or national GEWE initiatives on a global level. In this regard, throughout the text, I will explore the different interpretations of formal vs. informal forms of volunteering and political engagement as they relate to the way that women all over the world reinterpret 'power' and challenge the status quo in order to build a more inclusive and sustainable future for generations to come.

4.1 Bringing Awareness to the Cause

One of the most effective ways to bring about large-scale political change is by informing the public and bringing awareness to the issues for which political actors are advocating for. In this regard, IDVs are most helpful as they provide social support through role modelling, mentorship, and workshops that enable women's political engagement to flourish in their respective communities.

In recent years, communication technology (whether through the widespread use of the internet or the expansion of social media applications) has enabled us to have access to information from a wider distance and at a more rapid pace. As a result, international and national advocacy efforts have shifted to the digital space. In this regard, IDVs provide digital marketing assistance for numerous campaigns and capacity building initiatives aimed at bringing awareness on gender-related issues in a way that integrates these perspectives into everyday local activities. Social media advocacy increased the reach of local socially and politically engaged women's causes, thereby increasing their ability to place the need for an acknowledgement of women's equal rights and women's economic independence on wider platform (Schmid et al. 2008). This has the effect of calling upon local and national political representatives to respond to their needs by placing gender-related issues firmly on the agenda by working together with women's organizations to formulate policies that would help achieve gender equality in all sectors.

In Ghana, a local actor remarked: "[most] of [their] international volunteers supported [them] to use social media to highlight the issue of women in [their] work." Similarly, another local actor from Tanzania adds:

[the] digital marketing was [a volunteer]'s idea. She participated on these programs on building capacity on gender and training on standards. It enhanced marketing. Specific tools on the social media, so much of IT. Like, teaching people how to do sponsored ads. How to design their ads, how to customize their ad to be seen in a specific environment to reach specific people.

IDVs also provide psychosocial support to women in the form of mentorship and role modelling. This useful input exposes the local public to a diversity of perspectives on women's rights and gender relations, which effectively elevated the existing efforts of women's social, economic, and political organizations.

In Malawi, a female senior staff member at an international humanitarian organisation pointed out:

the fact that [they] have volunteers that are women in itself is a positive attribute because [she is] hoping that by a representative being a woman, by a protection officer being a woman a small refugee girl sitting in the camp would say 'I want to be that woman', and that alone is the perception gone that women cannot be leaders, women can not be bosses or women can not do this.

This interviewee added that volunteers have "a positive impact on the community regardless of [their] race or [their] gender."

Similarly, in Kenya, a male senior staff member at a community centre says that mentorship provides

psychosocial support to these [local] women, [since] these are women who used to think that they are down [low self-esteem] whatever so they used to kind of come [volunteers] make some kind of jokes or give stories, you see such kind of thing and then [local women] feel motivated and even they get a lot of energy to do what they want to do.

This form of support provided by IDVs has a lasting and transversal effect on participants as it enhances their ability to tackle many challenges related to GEWE on both a professional and personal level.

4.2 Providing Empirical Evidence to Enhance Women's Empowerment

On a more practical level, IDVs also apply a more participative approach to development by providing political support and opportunities to enhance economic empowerment for women. Volunteers work alongside women through training sessions and workshops, which led to an increased mobilization and participation of civil society on gender related issues.

One IDV based in Senegal is said to have been:

given the task of setting up the monitoring at the level of each member-State in order to develop the national action plan, because [the organization] already have a canvas for the development of the action plan, which the country adopts according to the realities on the ground. [The volunteer] shared the draft of the plan of action for the monitoring mechanism that must be put in place in terms of reference, it also follows until these two products exist in each country.

In Malawi, during a community level election an international volunteer is said to have been "quite instrumental together with some of the nationals to ensure that nominations were equal for men and equal for women, different ballots for men as well for women so that [they] could have equal presentation." This supports the notion that IDVs also supply local organizations with empirical evidence to support the need for women's empowerment and political leadership. It demonstrates a joint advocacy effort between international and local actors in the pursuit of gender equality.

In Senegal, a program director for a local women's rights organization network acknowledged that a female IDV's input enhanced their gender strategy, capacity-building by contributing to the development of the legal tool: "Additional Act for Equality of Rights between Women and Men in the CEDEAO space." Further, this IDV also contributed to "the capacity-building of member-State organisations, in trainings that [they] had to organise for the member organisations and even for [their] staff."

In Uganda, a female IDV "decided to write a paper and after three years [of volunteering] she came back with a paper and research, and she's been able to create a program to [prevent] that violence in [precarious] settings."

In Malawi, an IDV conducted an audit on how recruitment of staff is focusing on gender equality. The interviewee noted that the audit's final report "can be used in the planning and even justifications in the creation of some positions and even on how [local employers] can improve gender equality interventions in various sectors." As a result, the development of knowledge helped create "baselines for gender disaggregated data baselines and monitoring and evaluation."

This political support provided by IDVs enabled local organizations to receive the attention of governmental representatives who are better equipped to thereafter provide support on GEWE and appeal to the general public by utilizing their state legitimacy to legitimize the call to action. This shift then has a domino effect on both a local and global level, which we will explore in the upcoming section.

4.3 The Glocalization of Gender Equality

Globalization has increased local and international communities' interconnectedness which has helped facilitate the pursuit of gender equality on a global scale. Yet, the input of local civil society remains fundamentally instrumental to the execution of development activities. This justifies the formulation of NGO networks that coordinate their collective development efforts in a way that accommodates the needs of both the international and local participants (Kamruzzaman 2018). It also highlights the interdependence between global and local frameworks. However, many local, regional, and national initiatives that encourage women's political representation and participation (through politics and otherwise) have been put in place long before the arrival of IDVs. International institutional policies and frameworks are said to have provided a source of inspiration for local gender equality and women's empowerment initiatives. Many gender mainstreaming programs and policies are adapted to local frameworks to stimulate women's political participation and advocacy efforts. "We share similar [gender-related] views than that of the international community, here in Africa," remarks a Senegalese female senior member of a regional economic network. This interviewee explained further that the "powerful civil society organizations" address inequality by aligning interventions and subsequent indicators with international indicators as outlined in the UN's Sustainable Development Goal #5 and international conventions such Convention on the Elimination of all Forms of Discrimination Against Women (CEDAW) using these frameworks as references in interventions.

In addition to international influence, there is also strong local support for political participation. In Senegal, for example, gender parity is a requirement during elections:

> *Senegal is one of the few African countries to have signed the Total Power Parity Law on election-related instances, which means that in all election processes, the number of women must be equal to that of men, even if there are a few regressions on the part of the General Assembly, but at a certain point, we were almost at a level of total parity," according to the director of an employment agency in Dakar's outskirts.*

Signed in 2010, this law "obliges all political parties to place women and men in an alternating matter on candidate lists, aiming at a male-female ratio of 50%" thereby institutionalizing the equal representation of men and women in all governing bodies" (Tøraasen 2017: 2).

Moreover, in many countries where partner organizations operate, the state constitution reserves "special seats...for marginalized groups [such as] ...women as well as the youth," as noted by a senior staff member at a development NGO in Kenya.

Political mobilization is an essential step to the empowerment of women as it allows them to have access to a larger platform where they are able to express their needs and desires. IDVs support in the formulation of similar legal and political has opened up a space for local actors to inscribe their development goals in the code of law. However, not all GEWE initiatives take place in a formal structure, as we'll see in the next section, sometimes political moves can be undertaken outside the realm of politics.

4.4 Valuing 'Informal' Volunteering

Political engagement does not always have to be through the domain of high politics, it also implies leadership roles within existing framework linked to economic governance, women's leadership, and representation to name a few. Despite the recent institutionalisation of gender parity in formal government bodies, women's social mobilization is equally effective through grassroot organizing. In fact, women's associations often substitute the lack of state welfare and wanning resource allocation by providing the social servicing and the tools necessary for women to empower themselves (Tripp 1994: 108).

A local development actor in Vietnam remarked that the implementation of public servicing is waning in certain areas: "The overall problem of Vietnam is that we have laws, but the implementation is bad, and it doesn't really work very well when we come lower and lower levels." This form of social and political assistance can be described as 'informal volunteering' as it is not coordinated by a larger-scale network of governmental or NGOs but that delivers support to their community nonetheless. The fact that women participate in informal volunteering more often than men is a testament to the ways in which women are often excluded from the formal fabric of volunteer networks and lack access to public resources that would help give value to their invaluable work (Lough et al. 2018).

Despite claims of exclusionary membership, women's organization based on informal, communal, political, and economic linkages have proved to be anything but biased. Many volunteer initiatives by local women's organizations are unique in that they are able to mobilize women of various backgrounds under a common objective, regardless of their ethnicity, religious affiliation, or socio-economic level (Tripp 1994). These local women's associations' unique political engagement and advocacy are therefore essential to the advancement of GEWE on a more grassroots level.

4.5 Critical Reflexivity in International Relations

Despite the positive international support, many local development actors also express a need to restructure the Western feminist model in order to create authentic frameworks, reflective of local dynamics, allowing for an adaptive strategy to enhance local women's political agency. This recalls the need for critical reflexivity in the exchanges between international and local actors (Collier/Muneri 2016). It is important to make an explicit effort to decolonize the practice and the space in which development efforts are taking place. In order to better service the communities the international support is intended for, IDVs are advised to recognize their position of privilege by reflecting on their positionality. This means critically reflecting on one's intersectionality, meaning one's social position within a collective or society as it relates to their race, ethnicity, faith, education, sexual orientation, income-level, geography, (dis)ability, etc. These social positionings outline the power relations that exist between or within groups and can be a definitive factor of influence over the outcome of a development initiative.

The interpretation of gender equality varies from one context to another. In Peru, for example, a female staff member at a development NGO says that their work focuses of gender equality and the promotion of Indigenous women's rights, a social group that face "a specific kind of discrimination, which a whole other thing to work on."

Additionally, in many contexts' local religious leaders and conservative groups who directly or indirectly reinforce the patriarchal gender norms pose a threat to feminist women's empowerment initiatives. Accounts of these obstacles were noted by local volunteers in Tanzania and Peru as a local actor in Tanzania points out that "[i]n rural communities, religious leaders have a lot of power and they can make change," while another remarks that "it is very challenging to change community traditional beliefs, so it is a process to bring feminism issues in the community." Similarly, a female staff member at a development NGO in Peru echoes these sentiments by mentioning that the most notable barriers to the achievement of their goals are posed by conservatives and fundamentalists and that their work focuses on "defending the gender focus that has started to be present in the State and to defend [their] rights from these fundamental groups."

Many local actors recommend that IDVs make an effort to adapt to local culture in order to create a framework that is reflective to local needs. Failure to do so could otherwise result in "culturally incongruous directives that fail to account for local social dynamics" (Lough et al. 2018: 69). A local development actor in Uganda mentions this during an interview:

The facts are real but the implementation in our culture has not worked. For example, when you talk of Canada and the USA or wherever we hear that rights are respected 100% but here you have to be patient. You have to be patient for the sake of your family, for the sake of your marriage, for the sake of your children. So here women tend to suffer for the sake of their marriage, our relatives and our children over their own empowerment and rights. I think it's problematic in terms of its implementation, as it doesn't take into consideration Ugandan culture. We do talk about gender and equality and feminism, but it remains problematic.

If gender equality is the ultimate goal, reciprocity is key. "Yes, it's 50/50. It's two-way traffic. That is something we have noticed. We learn from them a lot, and they learn from us a lot", summarizes a local development actor in Tanzania. Mutual support between international and national volunteers is essential to the cohesion of various development goals. When IDVs reflect on their positionality and seek out ways to adapt or adjust their vision of development to fit the context in which they work, they are essentially restoring the power of decision-making in the hands of local actors for whom the support is intended for. This essential reflection on the importance of equity in the distribution of power requires us to also critically rethink the very notion of power and the ways in which it is exercised in a variety of contexts and by a variety of actors.

5. Analysis

Gender Equality and Women's Empowerment initiatives draw attention to the power dynamics that exist within a society. Yet it is important to recall that power, as a means rather than an end, is relative, since it is expressed in various forms and results in a multitude of outcomes. When evaluating women's ability to exercise power, one must also consider the informal and immaterial or abstract tools women have access to, in order to draw a fuller, more holistic portrait of their empowerment of self and of others.

In a globalized world, the tremors of developmental trends can be felt in even the most remote settings. As a result, whether intentional or not, today's local initiatives oftentimes have a broader framework than their pre-globalization era predecessors. Just as women's influence has the potential to envelop an entire community, today, that community in question may also be subjected to the changes of a widening political and social landscape.

There are many advantages to this increased global interconnectivity. For one, it allows for the proliferation of international cooperation in the pursuit of common objectives, like that of GEWE. In fact, many local actors modelled their GEWE frameworks on gender mainstreaming initiatives like that of the UNDP and Canada's Feminist International Assistance Policy (FIAP). Globalization facilitates the creation of platforms of exchange between international institutions and local organizations that enables them to build upon existing frameworks with novel research and capacity-building support.

This support is greatly aided by the influx of IDVs who contribute to local initiatives through activities geared towards promoting the development of women's leadership. The joint effort of local and international actors adds value to the output of political training that eventually results in an increase of women's political engagement through advocacy, activism and political representation. International volunteers who provide the public platform to expand the reach of local initiatives they are assigned to effectively help amplify the voices of local women, granting them more visibility in spaces where they were otherwise overlooked or invisible.

Yet this ability to reach a wider audience with a higher degree of credibility inevitably comes from the fact that IDVs are often granted the privilege of existing as outsiders, as highly valued contributors to often complex social and political environments. It is for this reason, that local organizers often prescribe a thorough and critical self-reflection of international actors' power and privilege. Specifically, IDVs are asked to revaluate their preconceived notions of 'ideal' development orientations and the ways in which these practices are being implemented in foreign settings. They are asked to expel normative prescriptions from their development agendas in order to objectively assess the needs of local actors in the historical and present context in which they find themselves. In the specific target goal of GEWE, this means doing away with the Western-conceived individualistic conception of feminism and women's empowerment, in order to formulate a more communitarian approach to gender relations (Collier/Muneri 2016). Hence, the need for critical reflexivity among IDVs to more effectively contribute to a transnational feminist vision of development.

IDVs who critically reflect on their positionality in relation to the positions of the people they are intended to support can better identify the root causes of the issues and the practical strategies needed to tackle them. In Kenya, for example, inclusivity in the debate on women's political engagement and empowerment requires a reconfiguration of gender roles and gendered social expectations, which entails the necessary implication of local male actors as well (Collier/Muneri 2016). Likewise, interviewees in Peru highlight the need for an intersectional feminist lens including a deeper understanding of Indigenous women's unique struggle for gender equality, as they simultaneously face gendered barriers within their community and racial discrimination on a national level. Similarly, in Guatemala, critical reflexivity allows international volunteers to get a sense for the unequal relationship that exists between the national government and local population. Ultimately, IDVs' capacity to adopt a critical, objective, and multidimensional perspective on the objectives that local organizations are striving towards reinforces the reciprocity of this international exchange of knowledge and skills.

As IDVs embody reciprocal interactions with local counterparts, these local actors become representatives of their own vision of development by calling attention to the causes that affect their communities, which is, in itself, an exercise of political agency. In this way, women who engage in such development activities feel empowered as their own interpretation of reality is valued by their local and international peers. This form of empowerment creates a ripple effect throughout their community, as the empowerment of self provides the tools and creates an opportunity to indirectly or directly empower those around us (Parpart/Rai/Staudt 2002). This also recalls the notion of "the exercise rather than possession of power", which seeks to redefine contemporary power relations by doing away with normative interpretations of effective governance in order to recognize the valuable contributions of non-traditional models of leadership (Parpart/Rai/Staudt 2002: 4).

The capacity building activities local actors participate in with IDVs also coincides with the expansion of their own political output, whether it be through social advocacy or policy prescriptions (Schmid et al. 2008). For instance, this was the case for the partnerships established in Senegal, where IDVs were able to contribute to the formulation of the Additional Act for Equality of Rights between Women and Men within the Economic Community of West African States.

However, the output of women's political engagement remains subjective to the political makeup of their respective regions or countries. In countries like Senegal or Peru where decentralized political structures allow for an explicit differentiation of powers between local and national governing bodies, local governments find themselves lacking the necessary resources to address their respective population's needs and concerns. This is often due to "limited local taxing powers", which prevent local governments from accumulating sufficient public funds to create and maintain public goods and services (Devas 2005: 3).

At the same time, the double burden women carry as both reproductive and productive contributors to society makes them doubly reliant on social services, especially during periods of instability (Tripp 1994). As a result, the quantity and quality of social resources on a local level begin to wane and women are often the first to be affected. In sum, there is an indirect correlation between women's access to social, economic, and political support, or the lack thereof, and their overall community's ability to develop.

In this regard, women's informal labour is crucial to the development of communities that lack sufficient resources from their respective governments. As such, the social servicing provided by informal volunteers enable women to have access to the tools necessary to full and equal participation in governing bodies (Tripp 1994). The fact that women make up a large proportion of these informal volunteering networks means that these networks are more knowledgeable in the specific issues that affect women's livelihood and ability to develop. They become a vehicle of change that mobilizes women in their objective to uplift other women.

Furthermore, the vertical relationship to power that exists within formal political structures is not always reflective of many women's horizontal relationship to the populations they serve. The findings indicate that despite significant strivings to promote GEWE, these initiatives continue to advocate for women because of the implicit barriers that prevent women from fully engaging and participating in formal party politics; the political authorities that yield the most power within many societies.

The recent legislation that requires women to have an equal representation in political leadership does not always address the root causes of their access to the resources necessary to that ascension to political power. These barriers might include the unequal and gendered division of informal labour and their lack of access to tertiary education, which is often a requirement for many positions of power. This lacuna is the main motivator for many capacity-building activities geared towards the promotion of gender equality. They center the conversation on the need for equity rather than just equality, by addressing the root causes of women's disempowerment in order to enhance the skills, knowledge, and opportunities necessary to their empowerment.

6. Conclusion

The form in which women's political participation, activism and advocacy manifests is subject to the local or national political structure, as well as the shifts that take place in their environment. As such, no two models of political mobilization or engagement are the same. Sometimes, the implicit barriers that prevent women from exercising power (i.e., local religious or conservative groups) are particular to the society in question and are imperceptible to the untrained external eye. Hence, the need for international or transnational actors' constant adaptation to local contextual social and political issues.

Transnational relations transcend the limits of international borders and national governance. They encourage individual actors to take initiative and contribute to global development through global cooperation. However, in doing so, international development thinkers and practitioners must also be cognizant of the contextual elements that shape one's positionality and the privilege it may grant them.

Equality does not necessarily imply an erasure of difference. In fact, the universalist approach to international development has the potential to create the opposite effect. The normative prescription of feminist social and political mobilization, or development orientation in a broader sense, has the potential to increase inequality rather than reduce it since the value of a more mainstream perspective could outvalue a more intersectional rationale. In order to avoid this outcome, the framework GEWE initiatives must be adapted to the context in which they are being implemented.

In an increasingly globalized world, local issues can take on a global scale, and vice versa. It is therefore important, as transnational cooperation and relationship has proven to continue to build these links through an equitable exchange of knowledge, skills, and power. In the field of international development, many programs, practices, and processes of development have recently been depoliticized in the hopes of promoting a more liberally inclusive approach to global development. Still, the multiple axes of disempowerment or discrimination in many societies continue to pose barriers to equal access to political participation, especially for women.

While depoliticization represents a step in the right direction for the maintenance of global cooperation, the fact remains that the persistence of social issues (as apolitical as they may seem) stem from the excercise of political power, or more specifically, the lack thereof. The achievement of GEWE therefore depends on the achievement of women's political participation in order to draw a more authentic portrait of equitable development – one that considers the voices of all individuals and groups within a society. This entails a global cooperation between IDVs and local actors in their efforts of achieving such a feat, until it ultimately becomes the norm. Since gender equality implies a social shift, women who exercise their political agency and encourage their peers to the same are effectively shifting the power dynamics within their respective social structures.

Women are leading by example by playing an active role in the development of their communities and creating a legacy for future female leaders. IDVs are instrumental to that process. They bring awareness to the causes initiated by local organizations, they offer social support to local actors though mentorship, capacity-building and trainings, and they provide research assistance on local gender-related issues. All in all, their contributions to local development in a variety of global settings represents continuous renewal of transnational cooperation in the noble pursuit of gender equality and women's empowerment.

Bibliography

Collier, Mary Jane; Cleophas, Muneri (2016): A Call for Critical Reflexivity. Reflections on Research with Nongovernmental and Nonprofit Organizations in Zimbabwe and Kenya. In: Western journal of communication, vol. 80, no.5, pp. 638–658.

Devas, Nick (2005): The Challenges of Decentralization. International Development Department of the School of Public Policy. England.

Kamruzzaman, Palash (2018): Civil Society in the Global South. Abington.

Lough, Benjamin J.; Carroll, Margaret; Bannister, Thomas; Borromeo, Katrina (2018): The thread that binds Volunteerism and community resilience. 2018 State of the World's Volunteerism Report, https://doi.org/10.18356/14b33d1a-en.

Parpart, Jane L.; Rai, Shirin; Staudt, Kathleen A. (2002): Rethinking Empowerment. Gender and Development in a Global/Local World. London.

Patterson, Amy (2002): The Impact of Senegal's Decentralization on Women in Local Governance. In: Canadian journal of African studies, vol. 36, no.3, pp. 490–529.

Schmid, Hillel; Bar, Michal; Nirel, Ronit (2008): Advocacy Activities in Nonprofit Human Service Organizations. Implications for Policy. In: Nonprofit and voluntary sector quarterly, vol. 37, no. 4, pp. 581–602.

Tøraasen, Marianne (2017): Gender Parity in Senegal – A Continuing Struggle. https://papers.ssrn.com/sol3/papers.cfm?abstract_id=3648097 (19.08.2021).

Tripp, Aili Mari (1994): Gender, Political Participation and the Transformation of Associational Life in Uganda and Tanzania. In: African Studies Review, vol. 37, no. 1, pp. 107–131.

International Volunteers as Empowerment Agents: Challenges and Opportunities of IDV Contributions to Women's Empowerment Programs in Partner Communities

Pascale Saint-Denis

1. Introduction

In recent decades the term "empowerment" has become increasingly popular in development discourse, making its way to the top of the aid agenda. The growing prominence of empowerment programming has led to transnational actors engaging in programming intended to enhance empowerment among marginalized populations, or in some cases, development actors have been tasked with 'empowering others'. As 'empowerment agents', aid workers, including international development volunteers (IDVs), are actively involved in several strategies to promote local empowerment. The central focus of this paper is uncovering the nature of that empowerment work, and the successes and challenges associated with transnational actors in empowerment activities. Research drawing on 150 interview findings in 10 countries in the Global South uncovered substantial qualitative information about how partner organizations and recipient communities in the Global South understand empowerment and the contributions of IDVs as transnational aid workers in the promotion of gender equality and women's empowerment (GEWE) programming.

In this paper, I argue that the nature of the empowerment contributions made by IDVs is shaped by broader global priorities and strategies that focus on a limited understanding of empowerment. Specifically, I contend that the potential role of IDVs as 'empowerment agents' is limited because empowerment is defined in narrow terms around economic development rather than political change. While examples of political empowerment are observed in some countries, there is a tendency to limit empowerment in neoliberal and superficial terms, such as economic advancement rather than systemic changes. As such, the empowerment approach employed does not promote a transformational approach to power relations and can also perpetuate relations of inequality through the imposition of western values or approaches that may not be embraced locally. However, empowerment-related interventions offered by IDVs can also open spaces for new conversations, providing opportunities for shifts in behaviours and attitudes in local communities with respect to gender equality and women's rights. These shifts take the shape of formal and informal knowledge exchange experiences, alongside some of the perceived benefits of economic empowerment programs. These challenges and opportunities are examined in greater detail in the findings and analysis sections below. First, I will summarize the significance – and implications – of empowerment programming emerging from scholarly literature. I return to these debates in the analysis to situate the findings from this study in the broader debates about the nature and impact of empowerment programming. The paper will then conclude with some recommendations and strategies for IDVs to enhance their roles within empowerment programming, such as investing in relationship-building practices and being well-versed in the partner country's social and historical context prior to their arrival.

2.   Literature Review

Going back to its roots, 'women's empowerment' is an inherently political notion, "contingent on women organizing to demand and promote change" (Sen/Grown 1987: 22) regarding the "structures of gender subordination" (Sen/Grown 1987: 25). As goals and priorities shift within development practice, however, the conceptualization of 'empowerment' has become a catch-all term and even buzzword (Batliwala 2007; Cornwall/Brock 2005), frequently combined with 'gender equality' by development actors (Eyben/Napier-Moore 2009) as GEWE (gender equality and women's empowerment). The issue of 'empowerment' now being a loosely defined concept, and even tossed together with 'gender equality', is well exemplified by the fifth Sustainable Development Goal (SDG) implemented by the United Nations (UN). The title of the SDG in question, "Achieve gender equality and empower all women and girls", employs the term 'empower', but there is no specific sub-target dedicated to supporting women's political movements (UN 2020). This space for subjectivity that is allowed to exist in reference to the term across development organizations and agencies therefore poses a significant challenge for streamlining the empowerment programming agenda.

Although 'empowerment' initially evoked women's political mobilization, Eyben and Napier-Moore (2009) point to an additional modern significance attached to it: economic empowerment. As women's economic empowerment has gained prominence in intervention efforts, the "meanings of empowerment associated with solidarity and collective action are being crowded out" (Eyben/Napier-Moore 2009: 294). Stripped of its original political depth (Kabeer 1999; Batliwala 2007; Sen/Grown 1987), women's empowerment programming has been re-imagined to fit an economic model, wherein women in the Global South are provided with the tools and knowledge through a technical and skills-based approach to generate revenue, thus allowing them to have improved agency and empower themselves (Cronin-Furman/Gowrinathan/Zakaria 2017).

Women's empowerment programs, delivered with the support of international development volunteers (IDVs), are often predicated on the micro-level economic model, and the opportunities for IDVs to insert themselves in local communities and assume the role of 'empowerment agents' are numerous. From facilitating employment opportunities to business development activities (WUSC 2018; Cuso International 2020), IDVs are encouraged to share their technical know-how and capacities to help women lift themselves out of poverty by getting jobs, designing business models or monetizing hobbies. Although these programs can admittedly be life-altering for women at the individual or even community level, they are "isolated from any possibility of collective political action," thereby effectively "exacerbate[ing] [women's] depoliticization" and "limiting the ability to achieve long-term political solutions" (Cronin-Furman/Gowrinathan/Zakaria 2017:10). As such, while acknowledging that individual women or groups of women can reap decent economic and material benefits from such economic empowerment programs, they merely apply a bandage to larger systemic issues. Kabeer highlights in her interpretation of empowerment "the interdependence of individual and structural change in processes of empowerment" while stressing that "structures shape individual resources, agency and achievements" (Kabeer 1999: 461), indicating that changes in the collective's lives are enabled through structural transformations. Despite these aspirational goals of empowerment in theory, in practice, 'empowerment' remains a diluted notion as women's lives and their conditions of their work are actively being depoliticized. The structures that uphold systemic issues of gender-based violence, inaccessibility to quality health care and socio-economic injustice are not being dismantled, but rather, they are being mitigated or may even be reinforced, by development efforts. The paper thus examines the role of IDVs in supporting different notions of 'empowerment' in their collaborative work with partner organizations and communities in the Global South.

Qualitative interviews with partner organization staff and program recipients provide rich insight into the experiences of working with IDVs in GEWE programming. The qualitative inductive thematic analysis of the study's findings points to three frames of analysis: 1) conceptualizations of empowerment; 2) implications for sustainability (long-term potential); and 3) prospects for reinforcing systems of inequality.

3. Methods

Interviews were conducted in 2018 – 2019 with 150 partner organization staff in ten countries. Once all interviews were transcribed, data were coded to identify common themes throughout. Data were analyzed using discourse analysis. This paper also draws on data from two focus groups with direct beneficiaries of Peruvian partner organizations. The introduction to this special edition has more detailed information on the methodology for data collection and the analysis of findings.

4. Findings

Several significant findings emerged from the data that point to the principal contributions IDVs have made within local communities as empowerment agents. I first discuss the various positive behavioural and attitude transformations that have taken place with local community members as a result of IDV interventions. I then present the challenges associated with IDVs as empowerment agents in recipient communities.

4.1 Shifts in Behaviours and Attitudes

Respondents commonly identified behavioural and mindset transformations as a contribution of IDVs' engagement in empowerment programming efforts within the local communities. As empowerment agents, volunteers have contributed to changes that have taken place in direct recipients' attitudes regarding gender equality and women's rights. The contributions of IDVs include formal interactions and informal interactions including relationship building.

Organized activities such as workshops and training sessions with local women as part of empowerment programs allowed volunteers to share their knowledge on a wide range of themes such as women's health (particularly reproductive health), gender-based violence, education, and equity in the workplace. These spaces facilitated by IDVs allowed local community members to speak freely and reflect on these crucial topics. A staff member of a partner organization in Peru remarked how the volunteer had the capacity to fill in specific knowledge gaps in issues of gender equality as she "...manages very well the theme of everything that is gender equality, the gaps in gender as well, everything that had to do with the theme of household violence" which allowed her to develop and teach classes for a school of gender in collaboration with the partner organization. According to the interview respondents, the volunteers who designed and led such activities generally had some formal education or background in the field of feminist and gender studies. They also emphasized the value of involving male community members in these types of workshops and pieces of training to support pushing back on traditional gender roles and expectations. One male participant from a development NGO in Kenya stated how the training provided by an IDV in this area helped him become a better ally to women. He began by explaining why he personally benefited from the training, noting "I used to be that kind of traditional husband but this [volunteer] training really changed my approach and now I am a champion against such perceptions and there are many in this community who have embraced the value of having more independent and equal women."

One respondent from a Peruvian development NGO described the ease with which the IDV could translate academic feminist thought and theories into everyday conversations with their direct recipients. The participant explained that the work of translating concepts into daily activities is "an important challenge", adding that translating knowledge into daily life means considering gender relations and a "gender focus" in all relationships. IDVs are seen as transnational actors who can incorporate gender in their relationships "with other people, with our team, the litigations with the beneficiaries. It is noticeable that it is fluid for her."

The ways in which male community leaders treated women following collaborations with IDVs were said to have an especially positive influence on how other community members consequently treated women. The actions and words of these community leaders carry much more significance in their communities than those of international volunteers alone, as suggested by the following quote from a Malawian partner organization staff member who sees the importance of changes to mindsets of community members: "how the chief treats their women and how he does perform the gender roles, that can have more influence than [the] volunteer." The international volunteers whose placements focused on presenting information on taboo topics and prompting discussion in formal settings generally left a positive impression on beneficiaries and partner organization staff members. Respondents consider themselves to be more knowledgeable and comfortable discussing such topics and recognize their modified behaviours.

Participants repeatedly described the importance of day-to-day interactions and informal encounters with IDVs where they could converse candidly and discuss their personal lives with community members outside of partner organization programs were repeatedly reported by the participants. Such occasions included lunch meetings, sports, and other leisure activities. Creating these safe spaces was key to fostering trust between IDVs and the direct recipients, particularly the women, allowing them to share their lived experiences and be more open-minded to other's values and notions of womanhood and equality. The following quote from a Ugandan interviewee captures this mutual experience of relationship building: "... they [IDVs] freely interact with everyone and share their personal stories on their own experiences in life" and this is seen as empowering. When IDVs engage in "the daily interactions with the staff and other women, they can share that power of influence. So when they share their experiences, women are able to share back and based on those sharings interpersonally and learn from each other". These interactions are believed to have a significant impact on the participants and the community members. It is seen to enhance mutual learning and supports a mutually beneficial arrangement.

One Peruvian beneficiary also explained how the IDVs they worked with offered crucial support in their personal life outside of their work with the partner organization, which helped foster a strong bond between them. The friendship that emerged built between the IDV and partner organization staff member was viewed as highly rewarding. The participant highlighted how the IDV: "gives us advice, she helps us, she understood me, she helped me learned [sic] words I didn't [sic] understand. She helped me a lot by accompanying me in getting a job, when I got sick she accompanied me." The caring role of the IDV was considered important in both work and in personal spaces.

In contrast to the formal experiences of knowledge exchange, any volunteer with feminist values was considered capable of sharing these principles through relationship building, despite not having any education in feminist and gender studies. Other participants noted that while individual changes regarding feminist values and ideas of gender equality may not have been as prominent in their communities, the exposure to and interactions with volunteers still influenced some local women to think about pursuing new paths in their education and careers rather than continuing to live by the cultural gender expectations. This opinion was expressed by a staff member in a Kenyan development NGO in the following excerpt: "[The volunteers] won't make [the women] more outspoken, but they would make them to want to take an initiative to improve their lives like pursuing a diploma course...". The interventions by IDVs allow the community members to reflect on their options and create new opportunities for the girls in the community to consider applying for scholarships to go abroad for school". The impact is that "their mind is opened up; they are open minded."

This informal knowledge exchange was also not limited to the local women, as men and boys were also cited to have made strong bonds with male and female IDVs and experienced a change in how they perceive and perform gender roles. The following quote from a Malawian partner organization staff member reflects on how "... [the male volunteer] was a role model to the boys..." and encouraged them to take on tasks that defied conventional gender norms, such as cooking. They finally realized that "... nutrition issues are not only for the girls, [or for] women in the kitchen, it's for everyone."

The respondents additionally stated that those in the communities engaged in the different knowledge exchange experiences frequently shared their thoughts and reflections with other community members, particularly their friends and family. Opening this dialogue with others was considered paramount to making major strides towards the collective shift in mindset and mentality on women's rights and gender equality. One Peruvian beneficiary regarded this effect as empowerment and reflected on how it impacted her and those around her: "It could be that change that has impacted me so much, and I have been able to change and change the chip of others, empower other women only through discussion. They, in turn, empower their family."

Investing in building trust with partner communities was considered an effective method for IDVs to engage with beneficiaries and better carry out their placements.

4.2 Women's Economic and Material Gains

In addition to the changes in mindsets at the personal and community level, the interviewees often reported economic, and material gains as notable IDV contributions. As part of women's economic empowerment programming, IDVs provided female recipients services intended to generate revenue. Partner organizations expressed that IDVs participated in labour insertion initiatives with beneficiaries, such as connecting with local employers, working on CVs, and preparing interviews. Other projects focused on entrepreneurship to support women in developing their small businesses. IDVs provided capacity building and skills training activities that touched on communications, such as designing and maintaining websites and promoting businesses and business management, including finances, developing budgets, and keeping inventory. A Senegalese partner described how the contributions of volunteers in financial management helped local women develop their businesses in different sectors by "...[training them] on how to [introduce] revolving credit ... to develop tools that will allow them to properly manage their revolving credit" which led to them to "...[develop] income-generating activities."

IDVs also provided capacity building services tailored to the specific products of women-owned small businesses to boost product sales, such as in Nepal, where "... they taught packaging, how to do the marketing, they taught them for the product to...sell the product more than before because of the packing."

Partner organization staff emphasized how generating revenue acted as a catalyst for women's increased agency and independence in their households. Receiving an income as a result of their involvement with IDVs improved women's roles as decision-makers in their homes and increased their self-confidence. Further, some local women who benefitted from these programs shared what they acquired with other women in the community so that more women could earn a better livelihood. Such was the case in Malawi where some volunteers assisted in creating different products from what a beneficiary groups of mothers cultivated from their garden who "are now able to come up with different snacks and they sell them out there. And also then they are now going out, teaching other mother groups from other surrounding schools."

4.3 Challenges Associated with IDVs in Empowerment Programming

While the data point to numerous positive contributions of IDVs concerning their engagement in empowerment programming, partner organizations also brought up the challenges and disadvantages associated with hosting IDVs. The two main challenges that respondents discussed were the imposition of Western notions and ideals of feminism and fostering discomfort in the local communities by challenging gender norms. Multiple partner organizations spoke about how they hosted some volunteers who consistently applied the standards of feminism and gender equality from their home countries to their new surroundings. This disconnect was attributed by partner organizations to a lack of open-mindedness or understanding of country context and was considered to be very problematic in IDV behaviours. The following excerpts from Peruvian and Ghanaian development NGO staff, respectively, acknowledge the differences in gender equality and equity according to social context and how they are not interchangeable:

I think that you can't import the concepts of gender equity that Canada would have that already works in that theme, it can't be directly imported here. The social differences between a Canadian woman and a Peruvian Indigenous woman, it's like from a different planet.

I have heard people talk about sometimes, in their cultural orientation in thinking about the issue [of gender equality] they want to wholesale it [their understanding of gender equality] on you and not recognizing the fact that, there are cultural issues that need to be respected.

Another Peruvian partner brought up their experience of white feminist ideals from IDVs, stating that "...the initiative, the fights of women, they have to leave from the same communities, the same women. It is not good that [the volunteers] come with Western impositions, with Western feminism, white feminism." Attempting to impose Western conceptualizations of feminism and white feminism onto the local community members and within partner organizations also often led to unrealistic expectations and problematic saviour complexes.

Further, partner organizations reported that some of their IDVs made partner community members uncomfortable by challenging gender norms in a way that was considered disrespectful. These behaviours were generally exhibited by female volunteers who engaged in activities usually reserved for men, such as smoking and drinking. In other cases, female volunteers' clothing choices did not comply with the region's standards for how women dress, such as wearing short skirts and shorts. Some also insisted on discussing taboo subjects with very resistant groups, such as sex education, politics, religion, or gender equality in general. While these attitudes were probably typical in IDVs' home countries, they were considered improper or offensive in partner communities, especially by the local men. Partner organizations in Kenya frequently brought up this issue, one emphasizing how the community would reject the new ideas IDVs were trying to approach "...based on a single issue like [seeing the IDV] smoking..." or "...when [they] walk half [naked] like the way western countries are doing..."

By not adhering to the local norms of how women should dress and act, these female IDVs undermined their ability to build relationships with local men and women, which was thought to hinder the effectiveness of their placement's functions. Many partner organization staff communicated this issue to their international volunteers, who took the complaints into consideration and adjusted their actions, and others continued to disregard the discomfort of communities and partner organizations. It is worth noting, however, that in some cases, IDVs' privilege of being foreigners allowed them to push back on cultural norms and create a space for partner organizations to start a dialogue on issues they could not have previously discussed.

5. Analysis

To situate the impacts and challenges of IDVs detailed in the above findings within the literature, I will utilize the following three frames of analysis: conceptualizations of empowerment; challenges as they pertain to structural inequalities and colonial continuities; and opportunities for changing attitudes and behaviours. These will also be helpful in highlighting how this paper contributes to international volunteerism scholarship, specifically regarding impacts on women's empowerment programs in partner communities.

5.1 Conceptualizations of Empowerment

The study findings echo the literature regarding the different meanings ascribed to empowerment, as interviewees frequently used it in different contexts, thereby seemingly lending itself subjective to the speaker. The term was most often used to refer to women's self-confidence, agency, autonomy, or any general improvement in their quality of life. If we revisit the conceptualization of empowerment defined by Sen & Grown, it is meant to be an emancipatory movement; a means to mobilize to bring an end to women's subjugation (1988). IDV empowerment programming should then primarily consist of placements supporting women's roles in activism, advocacy, and public policy. Indeed, some partner organization staff members and beneficiaries asserted that international volunteers were active in the political sphere as part of their mandate by helping organize campaigns, conducting capacity building activities with women in decision-making bodies, and working with state institutions and civil society organizations to push for policy changes (see Mpogazi in this volume for examples of political empowerment).

However, the participants described a wide range of different empowerment programs put in place by Volunteer Cooperation Agencies (VCP) with other partner organizations who have different objectives, operations, and results depending on the program's design. Given the evolution of empowerment programming in intervention efforts documented in the literature, it is unsurprising that the most common empowerment programs addressed by participants consisted of women's economic empowerment and empowerment through knowledge exchange. Therefore, although there were IDVs who supported local women in pushing for systemic change, they were not as frequently discussed during the interviews focussing on economic empowerment compared to their participation in other empowerment programs.

In some partner countries, it can be drawn from these findings that there is minimal focus on activism and advocacy for women's rights as a part of economic empowerment programs than programs that can demonstrate short-term relief and benefits. As a result, programs that are meant to aid local women in the process of economically empowering themselves may be indivertibly keeping them from mobilizing and taking space in the political world. It also indicates that there may be misaligned understandings of empowerment across partner organizations, their programs, and, subsequently, their objectives.

5.2 Perpetuating Inequality and 'Ongoing Saviourism'

Opportunities to build relationships of solidarity exist in IDV programming. However, these fall short, in part because of the broader systemic inequalities that persist through colonial continuities, reinforcing ideas that women in the Global South need to be "saved" by their Global North (often) white feminist counterparts. Global North values and feminist priorities are seen, in many examples in the findings, to be part of a neocolonial agenda through which norms and attitudes are forced onto Global South partners (Cronin-Furman/Gowrinathan/Zakaria 2017). It can also be understood as a gendered white saviour complex or imperial feminism, "which uses Western social and economic systems to judge and make pronouncements about how Third World women can become emancipated" (Amos/ Parmar 1984: 7). Such mentalities of global sisterhood exhibited by white female international volunteers are well exemplified in this study as partner organizations frequently denounced white feminist beliefs and impositions of Western feminist values from IDVs. There is already an inherent power differential in the relationship between IDVs and community members from partner countries, generally just by virtue of IDVs originating from Northern countries. The power dynamics at play are then exacerbated when we consider the intersecting identities and experiences that may render specific populations more marginalized within the various systems of oppression. They can then be further worsened by a lack of knowledge that volunteers may have about the systemic challenges local women face, a lack of understanding of the broader country context and history, and the mismanagement of expectations of their impacts.

The belief that white women are the saviours of racialized women in developing nations further victimizes and essentializes Global South women. It also promotes "othering" while reinforcing the white saviour complex that dictates that these women must be saved from their circumstances and surroundings. This process is also characteristic of the longstanding concern of IDVs preserving colonial continuities by subjugating the other's needs and priorities with the righteousness of their own intentions and ideas of what resembles an equal, functioning society (Heron 2007). Consider the following excerpt from Cronin-Furman, Gowrinathan, and Zakaria that reflects this concept: "This focus on the evils of local cultures and traditions has long served as an argument in favor of intervention as a moral duty, incumbent on feminists who want other, lesser women to be empowered" (2017: 7). Motivations such as this one vilifies local cultures as a justification of IDV interventions and are tainted with the colonial mindset of importing and imposing "cleaner" cultural practices and beliefs. If international volunteers believe that it is their responsibility to empower Southern women through their altruism, then empowerment objectives will not be met and gaps in equality will be maintained. Moreover, while VSOs and partner organizations need to examine all IDVs' motivations for taking part in empowerment programs, sending organizations can also be complicit in perpetuating a very dangerous narrative if we look at how some volunteer-sending programs are sold to the Western public. More specifically, narratives that reinforce "othering", essentialize women, and contribute to white saviour rhetoric of "empowering Global South women", can be compared to more transformative marketing messages from IDV-sending organizations that promote a collaborative process of mutual learning and exchange.

Regardless of their good intentions to share their knowledge with local women and support them in the fight for gender equality, Global North women, particularly white Global North IDVs, may walk a fine line between trying to rescue and trying to support, and between harming and helping (Heron 2007). Diversifying and complementing North-South IDV models with other volunteer programming such as South-South or local volunteering can help to reduce power relations and to further dismantle structures of inequality. Other opportunities for building a collaborative and partnership-oriented approach to GEWE are outlined in Sadat's paper (this edition), who discusses strategies some partner organization staff employed to enhance dialogue and discussion around culturally appropriate GEWE strategies.

It is important to note that the partner organizations that did not identify as a feminist organization also did not discuss strategies to work closely with local feminist groups or women's rights organizations. Feminists in the Global South have mobilized efforts for local initiatives to advance women's rights and develop strategies for gender equality long before its recent prioritization in the Global North. Similar commitments to the promotion of gender equality exist within the partner organizations, where feminist women's rights partners have fought for gender equality and pushed for national governments to sign on to international commitments that align with gender equality goals. As these feminist movements already have long existed in host countries, the perceptions of outsider perspectives, the western imposition of feminist values, and gender equality norms may be misdirected at IDVs. Therefore, this sensibility may rather reflect the lack of collaboration between development organizations and women's rights organizations, which ultimately hinders the capacity to effectively align goals and collective understandings of crucial notions and themes.

Despite these important considerations and critiques noted above, local Peruvian beneficiaries did not perceive these dynamics with the IDVs they had been in contact with, but generally described their interactions with IDVs as equal relationships and friendships. The perception of IDVs held by local beneficiaries may be influenced by their engagement with diverse models of volunteerism. For example, around half of international volunteers in Peru were South-South volunteers from Latin America, and some were members of the Canadian Latin American diaspora. The beneficiaries did not report any problems of feeling inferior to any international volunteers, including white volunteers from Canada. They instead showed appreciation for the quality of the services they received and the commitment that IDVs showcased. Thus, it is essential that we recognize the agency of the partner communities and document their experiences in their own words to better consider the nature and impact of IDVs in women's empowerment programming. In addition, some of the concerns noted by partner organizations are based on projected or imagined reactions by beneficiaries.

5.3 Opening Spaces for Changes in Attitudes and Behaviours

The interview data also revealed insights pertaining to the implications for the sustainability of IDVs' impacts as empowerment agents. For the purposes of this discussion, sustainability in the context of international volunteering refers to the degree to which IDV contributions can generate long-term positive outcomes and benefits, mainly once they have left the country and are no longer supporting partner organizations. As the empowerment programs presented by partner organizations in interviews differ in model and design, the sustainability of IDVs' contributions facilitated by these programs also varies. Evaluating contributions entail multiple challenges such as measuring the reach of the impact, the efficacy of partner organizations to deliver their services, and the role of IDVs in the delivery of services.

Beneficiaries and partner organization staff members communicated how specific IDV contributions had a broad reach and managed to benefit individuals who had not even been in contact with the international volunteers. For instance, community members' mindset and behavioural transformations regarding gender equality and women's rights following interactions with the volunteers could be considered a long-term benefit. Respondents described that those who benefitted directly from informal and formal knowledge exchange commonly shared and replicated these practices within their circles to open a dialogue with friends, family, and other community members. Direct recipients felt more comfortable speaking to others about taboo topics such as feminism, gender-based violence, and equal rights. Notably, male recipients could subsequently identify and denounce inappropriate actions or comments from other men in the community, which is meaningful as they also hold significant influence over the men in their circles and together have the capacity to re-define masculinity. Direct recipients themselves became agents of change, even after the volunteers had finished their placements. As such, this ripple effect that emerges from the data indicates that there are indirect recipients further out into the community who profit from empowerment programs. Nevertheless, if IDVs cannot connect and form relationships with partner communities, this ripple effect will be stunted, such as in circumstances where IDVs disregarded local dress codes or imposed Western ideals.

Regarding capacity building activities for women's economic empowerment, numerous IDVs engaged in programs that supported local women by strengthening specific skillsets, finding employment opportunities, and managing their small businesses. As noted earlier in this paper, there are apparent, immediate economic, and material benefits for many women who participate in these types of programs. Despite these benefits, however, there is a risk that comes with such livelihood empowerment placements guided by short-term objectives, which is a possible dependency on DVs' services and support. Several Peruvian direct beneficiaries of economic empowerment programs indicated that they believed they would struggle to continue developing their skills once the IDVs they worked with completed their placements. This concern underscores the constant need for these empowerment agent placements to be filled and how the sustainability of economic empowerment outcomes is particularly fragile.

While these contributions have generally left positive impacts according to partner organization staff members and local beneficiaries, some functions will continuously need to be assumed by IDVs as the challenges they address in their placements can only be adequately fixed with action from State or local government. This shortcoming is especially true for vulnerable groups whose pressing needs must be met with systemic change. Skills and knowledge can be appropriated and replicated to benefit individuals and even communities in some cases, but they will not be the solution to high unemployment rates, high rates of gender-based violence and inadequate health and education systems. IDVs are thus limited as empowerment agents, and future scrutinization of empowerment programs objectives is necessary to evaluate how short-term results could be tied to partner organizations priorities regarding funding and donor relationships.

The interviews conducted with partner organization staff in the 10 countries included in this study and the interviews with local community beneficiaries in Peru provide a rich discussion of the opportunities and challenges that IDVs bring to gender equality and women's empowerment programming. There are clear concerns raised about issues that arise from perceptions of Global North feminist values and/or inappropriate presentations of gender roles. However, these concerns were discussed in relation to a broader set of opportunities that shape the way that relationships can be built over time through collaborative programming.

6. Conclusion

Overall, partner organizations and community members were mostly satisfied with IDVs' contributions to empowerment programming within local communities and cited several benefits of their engagement. Volunteers most commonly facilitated formal and informal knowledge exchange experiences which have been associated with modifying mentalities and behaviours regarding GEWE. As empowerment agents, the IDVs opened a dialogue and prompted conversations surrounding numerous taboo topics and influenced direct beneficiaries to adopt feminist values. In turn, numerous direct beneficiaries transmitted what they had learned to individuals within their sphere of influence, furthering the long-lasting effects of these benefits. Moreover, volunteers provided technical support as part of economic empowerment program placements, which has enabled local women to earn revenue through developing their small businesses and finding employment opportunities through labour insertion initiatives. These outcomes were then associated with improving women's status in their households and an increased sense of agency. However, the narrow conceptualizations of women's empowerment that guide the short-term objectives of economic empowerment programs are incoherent with long-term development efforts to address root causes of structural inequality.

Notwithstanding the positive impacts of international volunteers in GEWE programming, some partner organization staff members remain somewhat cautious of the presence and impact of IDVs due to a number of challenges and difficulties that were discussed in interviews and outlined in this paper. Notably, some IDVs were criticized for their Western beliefs of feminism and gender equality that were not compatible with the context of their host country. Partner organization staff conveyed that some volunteers were harsh to judge the socio-cultural reality of female community members and insisted on the morality of their beliefs as above that of the communities'. In a similar vein, numerous IDVs were said to be dismissive of local gender norms and expectations by engaging in inappropriate gendered behaviours or activities, ultimately offending local community members and causing tension. The analysis within shows how these challenges are results and symptoms of racial and gendered power dynamics manifested through a saviour narrative. However, the beneficiaries expressed far fewer concerns about IDVs imposing their values, raising questions about the perceptions held by partner organization staff. Further research is needed to explore this inconsistency in perspectives to better understand what are real and what are perceived impressions of IDVs engaged in gender equality and women's economic empowerment programming.

Partner organizations offer two recommendations to lessen the impacts of the abovementioned challenges and enhance IDVs roles as empowerment agents. First, partner organizations recommended that IDVs possess considerable knowledge of the host country's context, including its cultural history and social norms prior to their arrival (a theme that is common across several papers in this volume: see papers by Sadat, Rouhani, Mpogazi). Partner organizations should provide additional pre-departure training that focuses on country-specific information and language training, when necessary, as partner organization staff consider current pre-departure training to be inadequate for preparing IDVs for the field. Specifically, IDVs must be well-informed of the complex gendered dynamics of the communities. Second, in-country partner organization offices should give international volunteers more time upon arrival for cultural adaptation and acclimation to the new environment before beginning their placements. This time will also allow volunteers to begin investing in building relationships with the beneficiary community members, which will be central to mitigating the IDV saviour mentality. A third recommendation: to enhance the empowerment components of women's economic empowerment activities, IDVs and partner organizations need to collaborate with women's rights organizations and other organizations that are experts in political empowerment. Doing so will facilitate a deeper analysis of empowerment processes and contribute to broader political goals and addressing structural inequalities in line with the definitions of empowerment from the scholarship.

Bibliography

Amos, Valerie; Pratibha, Parmar (1984): Challenging Imperial Feminism. In: Feminist Review, no. 17, pp. 3-19.

Bandyopadhyay, Ranjan; Vrushali, Patil (2017): 'The white woman's burden' – the racialized, gendered politics of volunteer tourism. In: Tourism geographies, vol. 19, no. 4, pp. 644–657.

Batliwala, Srilatha (2007): Taking the power out of empowerment – an experiential account. In: Development in practice, vol. 17, no. 4-5, pp. 557–565, https://doi.org/10.1080/09614520701469559.

Cornwall, Andrea; Brock, Karen (2005): What do buzzwords do for development policy? a critical look at 'participation', 'empowerment' and 'poverty reduction'. In: Third world quarterly, vol. 26, no. 7, pp. 1043–1060, https://doi.org/10.1080/01436590500235603.

Cronin-Furman, Kate; Nimmi, Gowrinathan; Rafia, Zakaria (2017): Emissaries of Empowerment. Colin Powell School for Civic and Global Leadership. http://www.deviarchy.com/wp/wp-content/uploads/2017/09/EMISSSARIES-OF-EMPOWERMENT-2017.pdf (2.19.2021).

Cuso International (2020): Empowering Women and Girls. https://cusointernational.org/our-focus/empowering-women-and-girls/ (2.27.2021).

Eyben, Rosalind; Napier-Moore, Rebecca (2009): Choosing Words with Care? Shifting meanings of women's empowerment in international development. In: Third world quarterly, vol. 30, no. 2, pp. 285–300, https://doi.org/10.1080/01436590802681066.

Heron, Barbara (2007): Desire for development. Whiteness, gender, and the helping imperative. Waterloo.

Kabeer, Naila (1999): Resources, Agency, Achievements: Reflections on the Measurement of Women's Empowerment. In: Development and Change, vol. 30, no. 3, pp. 435–464, https://doi.org/10.1111/1467-7660.00125.

Sen, Gita; Grown, Caren (1988): Development, crises and alternative visions: third world women's perspectives. London, https://doi.org/10.4324/9781315070179.

United Nations (2020): Goal 5. Achieve gender equality and empower all women and girls. https://sdgs.un.org/goals/goal5 (2.22.2021).

WUSC (2018): Volunteer Reflections on Building Women's Economic Empowerment in Jordan. https://wusc.ca/volunteer-reflects-on-role-in-building-womens-economic-empowerment-in-jordan/ (28.10.2021).

CONCLUSION

The Intricacies of Transnational Relationships in the Promotion of Gender Equality and Women's Empowerment

Nnenna Okoli

1. Introduction

This special issue examined the exchange of knowledge and experiences and the relationships built in transnational spaces between international development volunteers (IDVs) and partner organizations (or volunteer receiving organizations) in the Global South. The focus of analysis running throughout this collection was an examination of the work of transnational actors in gender equality and women's empowerment (GEWE) programming.

The papers drew from a database of qualitative research conducted in ten different countries (Ghana, Kenya, Malawi, Tanzania, Senegal, Ghana, Nepal, Vietnam, Guatemala and Peru) by emergent and prominent researchers from the Global North and South between 2018 and 2020. The overall research design was collaborative, participatory and reciprocal, in that the knowledge and perspectives of Global South partner organizations were solicited from the initial planning stages to the final execution of the research. The research project also prioritized the development of budding scholars' research capacity through their participation in the creation of the research design, data collection, data analysis and the presentation of the findings. In this way, this special issue shifts the spotlight from the agency of actors in the Global North's to a (re)valuing of the voices and contributions of people in the Global South. It recognizes the value of mutual learning facilitated through international volunteerism programs to realize SDGs like gender equality.

The contributions in this collection drew from multiple theorical perspectives that share common analytical perspectives of women in development (WID), women and development (WAD), and gender and development (GAD). In their analyses of gender equality, the discrete papers employed discursive normative theory, identity-based theories, feminist theories, critical development theory, and the human capabilities framework. Drawing on these diverse but connected theories to explain qualitative research findings, contributors to this collection confirmed the significant multi-dimensional contributions that IDVs offer to realize GEWE targets in the Global South. Importantly, IDVs make these contributions through collaborative and generative interactions with partner organizations in line with transnational feminist values that eschew strict economic development in celebration of human and relational interactions.

2. Core Themes

The relational dimension of the transnational interactions between IDVs and partner organizations in the Global South fills an important gap in the scholarship, moving beyond a study of the experiences and impacts of international volunteers. Unlike most quantitative research on this subject, the collection's qualitative research methodology enabled the researchers to unpack the subjective meanings that partner organizations ascribed to processes, actions, interactions, and relationships with volunteers as they relate to GEWE programming. These interactions extended beyond the technical and "functional" revealing a deliberate cultivation of human relationships based on trust, inspiration and friendship in both formal and informal spaces. These interpersonal interactions greatly strengthened IDVs' contributions to gender equality outcomes.

Various case studies in this collection illustrated how IDVs' interpersonal relationships influenced their pursuit of gender equality targets. For instance, the relational complementarities of IDVs facilitated the acknowledgement and acceptance of alternative notions of womanhood and gender equality in the host communities while simultaneously informing the IDVs of cultural specificity and local context. The case studies also highlighted that the informal encounters and the exchange of personal intimate knowledge between IDVs and host communities greatly catalyzed the positive shift in local women's and men's perceptions of their rights and assigned gender roles.

On the other hand, these case studies also highlighted challenges that emerged from these interpersonal relationships across different cultural and geographic contexts. In cases where potential relationships of trust and respect were jeopardized by factors like IDVs' disregard for local culture and behavioral norms, communities were justifiably hostile and unreceptive of IDVs. As these case studies imply, volunteers with low levels of intercultural competence, empathy and recognition of cultural relativism consequently diminished whatever impact they could have made in promoting gender equality and empowerment in the communities where they served.

Other important insights offered by the articles in this special issue include the strength and value of Global South actors; the primacy of their agency; and the critical importance of their voice in their relations and interactions with IDVs, donor organizations, and other Global North partners. Evidence from this research highlights that the many benefits of these transnational relationships can be fully reciprocal, including contributions such as capacity building, knowledge sharing, intercultural learning, and innovation. They accentuate that Global South organizations are not simply recipients of funding, technical assistance, and the vessels of resources from the Global North; but they are also valuable contributors to the development of IDVs' skills and capacities.

Partner organization staff expressly underscored the advantages of hosting volunteers whose expertise and distinctive values on gender relations enhanced organizational perspectives and actions in pursuit of GEWE. They celebrated the genuine value of these relationships that were felt as mutually symbiotic and collaborative. This was particularly true in cases where both parties engaged in a partnership that upheld local organizational and communal principles and priorities – especially when local customs clashed with Western feminist ideals.

The findings also speak to literature on the intersections between gender mainstreaming, volunteerism, and international development. Gender has been mainstreamed to varying degrees in development organizations' structures, systems, processes, policies, and programs. However, its interpretation and implementation by development actors have varied and mostly produced disappointing outcomes. Using the Vietnamese case study, Lan Nguyen speaks to extant critical feminist criticisms of gender mainstreaming in development policy and practice. Partner organizations in this context either downplayed the important role of civil society in pushing the GEWE agenda or adopted a myopic conceptualization of gender equality. Central to this thesis was the neglect of the relational and structural dimensions of GEWE, and a focus on its instrumental and depoliticized form. In Vietnam, the existence of national pro-GEWE policies and the significant representation of women in the public sphere were erroneously equated with the realization of gender equality and empowerment. This superficial approach can be attributed to partner organizations' attempt to display some form of gender-sensitivity in their projects to strategically position themselves for continued receipt of donor funding. To the chagrin of critical feminists, this same approach tends to dominate development practice in the Global North.

Characteristic of mainstream development's conceptualization of empowerment, the version of empowerment described in this collection was often bereft of political elements necessary to transform oppressive gendered power relations and structures. For instance, Saint-Denis' analysis points to the subjugation of the inherently political project of empowerment to the neoliberal economic agenda through a narrow focus on assets and skills transfer to expand women's economic opportunities. Not to be mistaken, however, IDVs were able to harness their formal and informal interactions with beneficiaries of GEWE programs to encourage positive attitudinal and behavioural changes within communities, while also securing economic benefits for individual women.

Likewise, the paper by Tiessen, Laursen, Lough (with Mirza) elaborates on IDVs' contribution towards transformative social innovation and economic empowerment for women. This paper also addressed women's social vulnerabilities that are rarely covered in the literature, such as time poverty. In Tanzania and Ghana, IDVs recognized the unequal burden of unpaid domestic and care work on women's poverty due to its constraints on their opportunities for paid employment, skills training and education (UN Women, 2019). Hence, IDVs began to address these structural limitations by introducing equality-promoting programs such as child-care services during trainings and workshops to enable women to participate in GEWE programs.

IDVs further promoted women's political empowerment and collective mobilization by offering mentorship, motivation, and entrepreneurial and leadership training to women in the communities, as well as technical, research and advocacy support to partner organizations for political transformation. As Mpogazi emphasized throughout her paper, the efforts of IDVs working in partnership with Global South organizations helped to amplify women's political voice, capacities, representation, and collective participation. This was particularly evident in the case description of the network of councillors working in the district of Niayes (RCAN) in Senegal. Each of these activities served to enhance the visibility of the gender equality cause, buttressed the agenda for women's empowerment, and emphasized the critical importance of GEWE activities to policymakers.

In spite of the many contributions that IDVs make to GEWE programs, these improvements are often clouded by inter-cultural tensions between IDVs, their host organizations, and communities. Mirroring post-colonial feminists' critiques of Eurocentric feminisms, findings from Peru, Ghana and Kenya all highlight the tendency of IDVs to universalize and homogenize the oppression of women across racial and cultural categories while simultaneously essentializing "Third World women" as victims of their oppressive patriarchal cultures. Communities' resistance to IDVs' foreign ideas on ideal gender relations were prevalent in most of the countries represented in this collection. At the same time, Sadat's findings suggest a potentially different outcome resulting from these intercultural differences. This paper found that IDVs may be strategically positioned to influence gender norms and stereotypes because communities may be more receptive to gender equality messaging and advocacy coming from external agents like IDVs.

Points of cultural friction were particularly evident in cases where female IDVs contravened their host communities' traditional gender norms pertaining to women's responsibilities and mode of conduct. Interestingly, such tensions were far less observable when male IDVs pushed back on traditional gender roles and stereotypes. As Shahadu Bitamsimli highlighted in his paper, partner organizations painted men as strategic allies in reforming patriarchal gender norms to ensure the success of GEWE initiatives. The cross-cultural interactions and exchanges between male IDVs and their host communities created space for imagining alternative forms of gender division of labour in situations where unpaid care and domestic work were more evenly distributed between women and men. By embodying unconventional masculinities that transcend patriarchal cultural norms, male IDVs served as models for male community members to advance the goal of gender equality and empowerment. Considering men's general resistance to gender mainstreaming policies and programs (see Parpart, 2014), men's reorientation and inclusion in GEWE programming is beyond integral to the success and sustainability of these programs. Getting buy-in from men to advance and advocate for GEWE programming effectively mitigates resistance and resentment among men that would otherwise be excluded.

Another important highlight of the papers in this collection is the exertion of agency by Global South partner organizations working with IDVs. Previous literature already acknowledges that IDVs are instrumental in building the capacities of partner organizations through the transfer of skills, knowledge, and resources essential to the successful implementation of GEWE programs. However, Sadat provides a new perspective by emphasizing the reciprocal nature of capacity building and capability development; such that benefits accrue to both IDVs and partner organizations. In this way, asymmetrical power relations are evaded. Through reciprocity and partnership-based relationships, partner organizations were able to provide localized and contextualized knowledge on gender issues while correspondingly enjoying increased organizational efficiency and innovative ideas as a result of their collaborations with IDVs. As Rouhani illustrates, the transnational interactions between IDVs and partner organizations facilitate the creation of novel ideas and enhance the latter's strategies to dismantle structural barriers to women's rights through the synthesis of cross-cultural ideas on gender equality. Hence, the transnational space in which IDVs and partner organizations operate is characterized by a multi-dimensional flow of ideas, resources and skills that mutually enhances the cosmopolitan identities of both parties and flattens power differentials. Within this space of transnational interaction and reciprocity, Global South organizations were able to exercise their agency. Findings buttress the conclusion that their locally informed voices on gender issues were respected by IDVs as valuable and insightful.

The agency of Global South organizations was also evident as they navigated the structural inequalities stemming from overreliance on donor funding for their operations. Laursen delved into the negotiation, compromise, resistance, and decision-making processes of these organizations in relations to the compatibility of donors' feminist objectives with their organizational values, interests, and priorities. While Feminist Foreign Policies have decisively altered donor-recipient relationships by intensifying the (sometimes unfavorable) GEWE conditionalities attached to aid, Global South organizations have employed various tactics to assert their autonomy where possible. The organizations' preservation of their own ideologies, values, and objectives at the expense of donor funds reflects their preference for greater autonomy and ownership of their programs. Findings from this paper suggest that these choices were largely determined by donor requirements and expectations; donors sought to fund potential recipients based on good fit and compatibly with their cultural norms, regardless of their innate capabilities. These findings further highlight the importance of cultural awareness and sensitivity on the part of donors and IDVs in their relations with partner organizations in the Global South

3. Implications

Taken together, the papers in this collection contribute to our knowledge on the unique roles of IDVs and Global South partner organizations as transnational actors in international development. The discrete papers each pay attention to the intricacies of the transnational relationships between IDVs and partner organizations. By analyzing these intricacies, they consequently uncover a form of power relations that transcend dominant conceptions of international development volunteering. In terms of capacity building for example, the collection shows that capacity development is jointly shaped by both IDVs and partner organizations; such that there is a mutual and enriching exchange of skills and knowledge between both actors.

The analyses also recognize partner organizations as active transnational actors with distinct experiences, perceptions, and expectations. These partners are often assertive in planning and implementing GEWE programming to affect gender equality outcomes. Although the existing literature has mainly privileged Northern organizations' judgements of the impact of international volunteerism, this collection offers more inclusive insights into the experiences of partner organizations. It demonstrates that partners are not merely beneficiaries but are active contributors to transnational spaces.

This process brings a more dynamic lens to our understanding of the interpersonal relationships between IDVs and partner organizations that are pivotal to understanding the extent of IDVs' contributions to the processes and outcomes of the GEWE programming. This lens also highlights the distinctive contributions of international development volunteering as a model of transnational relations to the diffusion of norms, ideas, information, skills, and principles geared towards the transformation of gender relations and structures in the Global South. Although the specific contexts differ, the collection provides many detailed accounts of the dynamics of GEWE programming in the Global South to illustrate these points across diverse communities. These accounts illustrate important messages such as the negotiation of power and interests between Southern partner organizations, Northern donors, and IDVs; the cultural tensions inherent in the implementation of GEWE programs; the setbacks and successes in achieving transformation in gender relations; the process of engaging with boys and men in pursuit of GEWE; and the prominent role IDVs can potentially play in all of these processes.

4. Recommendations

The nuanced complexity, merits, and limitations of the transnational interactions and relationships between IDVs and partner organizations have been illustrated well throughout the papers. From the evidence presented, several recommendations emerged to enhance the impact of IDVs in facilitating GEWE programming and development outcomes broadly.

Perhaps the most glaring concern articulated by partner organization staff was the cultural friction that characterized IDVs' promotion of gender equality. The papers point to tensions surrounding IDVs' imposition of feminist standards that contravened established customs and traditions, as well as their ignorance of the political, economic and social contexts that implicitly defined gender relations of their host communities. Even worse was the blatant dismissal and disrespect of host communities' cultures as inferior and the neglect of the internal dynamics of communities which they seek to transform positively.

To ameliorate this less than savoury side of this relationship, volunteer sending organizations must do better to prepare volunteers for their engagements with cultures of difference. IDVs can be better prepared by studying the geographical, political, socio-economic, and cultural contexts of their placement communities before arriving. When they arrive, their placements can be structured to ensure that they are continually receptive to further experiential knowledge on the gender norms that they seek to transform. Understanding local communities' interpretations of GEWE and engaging with the scholarly and activist works of feminists in the region would help IDVs frame their contributions to best suit their cultural context. For instance, there is a significant and rich literature on African feminisms that embraces a more conservative approach to GEWE while retaining traditional African values (Nnaemeka 2004; Nkeala 2016). To further learn from local contexts, IDVs can also link with locally based women's rights organizations and feminist organizations who can help communicate cultural realities while also helping local partners interpret the programming activities of IDVs using local gender expertise.

Paramount to helping IDVs' develop greater cultural competence and a respect for relativism, they must be encouraged to engage in critical reflexivity on the power differentials between them and their host organizations and communities. Taking these power differences into account, IDVs can be more sensitive and respectful of local norms before proposing what and how change to gender dynamics should occur. The creation of space for critical reflection is not only consistent with ethical practice, it also carries the capacity to increase the impact and value of IDVs' presence in their host organizations and communities. As a further benefit, a clear respect for local priorities would endow GEWE program beneficiaries with a greater sense of empowerment because GEWE initiatives would not appear arbitrarily alien but would effectively reflect their own perceptions and meanings of gender equality and women's empowerment. Taking these actions, IDVs can aspire to emulate the example of the following volunteer working in Tanzania:

> *She is a person that used to reflect before speaking; to ask before sharing [...]*
> *She was a person that was ready to learn in every moment so, it was very difficult for her to [do or say] something that may result to conflict because she was very conscious to understand the values, the community situation, before she speaks, before she acts, before she shares anything... (see the paper in this collection by Tiessen, Laursen, Lough, with Mirza)*

The importance of cultural sensitivity for the effective delivery of GEWE programming cannot be overemphasized. After all, IDVs' expertise and innovative ideas would serve no use if they were rejected outright by the communities they seek to help.

Findings from this collection also emphasize that the length of IDVs' placements is crucial to successful cultural immersion. If IDVs are to reasonably understand the cultural contexts and contribute meaningfully to gender equality and empowerment, significant time must be allowed for IDVs to first learn about the culture and context before acting or speaking on gender issues in the host communities where they are placed. These benefits of cultural immersion would not be feasible with short-term placements of less than three months; thus, longer placements are preferred. When local trainings are paired with cultural immersion of a sufficient duration, many of the potential problems evident in these papers could be avoided. Furthermore, these measures would help ensure strong rapport and trust between IDVs and their hosts.

Perhaps the most important theme, with clear implications for practice, is the importance of reciprocal learning and intercultural exchange between IDVs and Global South partner organizations. Much emphasis has been placed on the need for IDVs to be cognizant of cultural specificities of their host communities. However, partner organizations can also benefit from understanding the contexts that frame IDVs' feminist values. When Northern IDVs and Southern partners come together with minds open, ready, and prepared to learn, they will discover mutual understanding and genuine shared insights.

Although research that informed this collection was gathered in the South as an evaluation of North-South volunteer initiatives, Global South partners would also benefit from *exchange* opportunities to travel to the Global North. Transnational exchanges characterized by mutual cultural immersions from South to North can aid critical reflections on the distinct cultural practices in the Global North. This would allow Southern sojourners to critically appraise how their gendered relations intersect and diverge along lines of power and cultural expectations.

5. Bibliography

Nkealah, Naomi (2016): (West) African feminisms and their challenges. In: Journal of Literary Studies, vol. 32, no. 2, pp. 61-74, https://doi.org/10.1080/02564718.2016.1198156

Nnaemeka, Obioma (2004): Nego-feminism: Theorizing, practicing, and pruning Africa's way. In: Signs: Journal of Women in Culture and Society, vol. 29, no. 2, pp. 357-385, https://doi.org/10.1086/378553.

Parpart, Jane L. (2014): Exploring the transformative potential of gender mainstreaming in international development institutions. In: Journal of International Development, vol. 26, no. 3, pp. 382-395, https://doi.org/10.1002/jid.2948.

ABOUT THE AUTHORS

Dr. Rebecca Tiessen is a Professor in the School of International Development and Global Studies and 2021 Recipient of the Excellence in Research Award for the Faculty of Social Science at the University of Ottawa. Her research explores the intersection of transnational action, feminism, gender equality and international development.

Dr. Benjamin J. Lough is a Professor at the School of Social Work and Director of Social Innovation at the Gies College of Business, University of Illinois at Urbana-Champaign, USA. He also holds positions as Senior Research Associate with the Center for Social Development in Africa, University of Johannesburg, South Africa, and Faculty Director of International Service at the Center for Social Development, Washington University in St. Louis, USA.

Tiffany Laursen is a PhD candidate at the University of Illinois at Urbana-Champaign. Her research interests (specifically citizen engagement in international poverty, grassroots social innovation, and strategies NGOs use for social change in the Global South) are influenced by, and intersect with, experience working in eight countries. Tiffany earned her Bachelor's in Leading International Social Change from SUNY Empire State College and her Master's in International Relations/Development from Harvard University.

Khursheed Sadat is a PhD Candidate in the School of International Development and Global Studies at the University of Ottawa. Currently her research centers on understanding the gap between feminist theory and its translation into development policy and programming by mainstream development organizations.

Leva Rouhani is a feminist international development educator, researcher, and consultant, specializing in gender equality and women's empowerment issues. For over 13 years, Leva Rouhani has worked with Canadian and International organizations on women's rights issues. Leva has worked and lived in sub-Saharan Africa, Middle East, South Asia, and Latin America/Carribean. She currently lives in Ottawa, Ontario, Canada where she is conducting research on the impact of COVID-19 on gender equality. She completed her PhD in the Education Faculty at the University of Ottawa in May 2021.

Somed Shahadu Bitamsimli is an international doctoral candidate from Ghana completing his PhD in International Development Studies at the University of Ottawa, Canada. In 2020, Somed received the International Development Research Centre (IDRC) Research Award to conduct research on engaging men and boys in gender equality programming in Ghana.

Lan Thi Nguyen is Ph.D. Candidate at the Asian Institute of Technology, Thailand, and currently a Lecturer in Gender and Development Studies at Vietnam Women's Academy, Vietnam. Her research interests cover gender equality and social inclusion at work, gender and technology, technology-facilitated gender-based violence against women and LGBTQI people using feminist framework and intersectionality in the context of Vietnam and Asia. Lan earned her Bachelor's in language teaching at Vietnam National University, Hanoi and her Master's in Development Studies from the University of Melbourne, Australia.

Rika Mpogazi graduated from the International Development & Globalization program at the University of Ottawa in 2021, where she also participated in research-related work in Brazil and Senegal. Apart from her writing and editorial work at online publications like *Ignio*, The Fulcrum and TRAD magazine, Rika currently works at Plan International Canada, a global organization dedicated to advancing children's rights and gender equality.

Tabitha Mirza is a graduate of the University of Ottawa with a Bachelors in Social Sciences in International Development and Globalization. She currently works for the Canadian Women's Chamber of Commerce. Previously, Tabitha worked for the Tanzania Tourist Board in partnership with the World University Service of Canada promoting economic empowerment opportunities for women and youth in Tanzania's tourism, media, and agriculture sectors.

Pascale Saint-Denis is a graduate student in the Master of Arts in Science, Technology and Society at the University of Quebec in Montreal and recipient of the Social Sciences and Human Research Council of Canada award. From 2020-2021, she was a Research Awardee in the Education and Science Division of the International Development Research Centre (IDRC).

Nnenna Okoli is a PhD student at the University of Ottawa who analysed data and helped synthesize the collection in the concluding paper. Her research is focusing on gender mainstreaming of social protection programs in Nigeria.